T

Marjorie Kinnan Rawlings's Cross Creek Sampler

UNIVERSITY PRESS OF FLORIDA

Florida A&M University, Tallahassee
Florida Atlantic University, Boca Raton
Florida Gulf Coast University, Ft. Myers
Florida International University, Miami
Florida State University, Tallahassee
New College of Florida, Sarasota
University of Central Florida, Orlando
University of Florida, Gainesville
University of North Florida, Jacksonville
University of South Florida, Tampa
University of West Florida, Pensacola

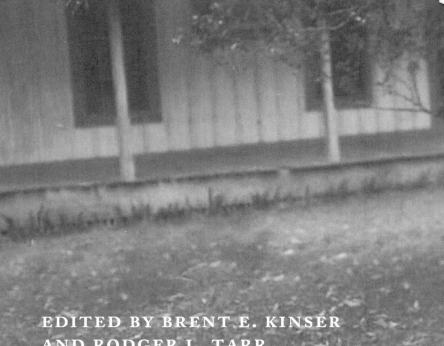

EDITED BY BRENT E. KINSER
AND RODGER L. TARR

University Press of Florida Gainesville Tallahassee Tampa
Boca Raton Pensacola Orlando Miami Jacksonville Ft. Myers Sarasota

Marjorie Kinnan Rawlings's Cross Creek Sampler

A BOOK OF QUOTATIONS

16 15 14 13 12 11   6 5 4 3 2 1

Library of Congress Cataloging-in-Publication Data

Rawlings, Marjorie Kinnan, 1896–1953.

[Selections. 2011]

Marjorie Kinnan Rawlings's Cross Creek Sampler: a book of quotations / edited by Brent E. Kinser and Rodger L. Tarr.

p. cm.

Includes bibliographical references and index.

ISBN 978-0-8130-3724-0 (acid-free paper)

I. Kinser, Brent E. II. Tarr, Rodger L. III. Title.

PS3535.A845A6 2011

813.'52—dc23   2011018966

The University Press of Florida is the scholarly publishing agency for the State University System of Florida, comprising Florida A&M University, Florida Atlantic University, Florida Gulf Coast University, Florida International University, Florida State University, New College of Florida, University of Central Florida, University of Florida, University of North Florida, University of South Florida, and University of West Florida.

University Press of Florida

15 Northwest 15th Street

Gainesville, FL 32611-2079

http://www.upf.com

For Froggy and Stinky,
Two Women
of Unusual Distinction
and Patience

The universe breathed, and the world inside it breathed the same breath. This was the cosmic life, with suns and moons to make it lovely. It is important only to keep close enough to the pulse to feel its rhythm, to be comforted by its steadiness, to know that Life is vital, and one's own minute living a torn fragment of the larger cloth.

Rawlings, *Cross Creek*

Contents

Introduction

The Defense

Marjorie Kinnan Rawlings (1896–1953) was a gifted writer who during her lifetime garnered myriad prizes for her fiction. She was especially appreciated for her descriptive powers, her character portrayals, and her penchant for moral sentiment. Her novels were best sellers; her short fiction was read widely. She was considered by Charles Scribner III as one of Scribners' foremost authors, and she was held in the highest esteem by the fabled editor Maxwell E. Perkins. Her work continues to enjoy universal appeal and has been translated into nearly every major foreign language. Her most famous works, *The Yearling* (1938) and *Cross Creek* (1942), have not yet gone out of print.

In addition to Rawlings's professional success, her personality was larger than life. Her friendship was valued by extraordinary individuals as diverse as Owen D. Young, American ambassador and industrialist; Pearl Primus, dancer, choreographer, and anthropologist; and N. C. Wyeth, artist and illustrator. She fished with Ernest Hemingway in Bimini; she lunched with F. Scott Fitzgerald in Asheville; she got drunk with Thomas

Wolfe in New York; and she lifted sacred glasses with Dylan Thomas at her home in Crescent Beach, Florida, just months before they both died. She hunted with Julia Scribner, whom she considered her "goddaughter"; she squired the youthful Andrew Wyeth around Cross Creek, before he became the "painter of the people"; and she caught rattlesnakes with the famed herpetologist Ross Allen. Rawlings moved easily among the rich and the famous. She visited the White House as a guest of Eleanor Roosevelt, and she partied in Hollywood with the moguls of MGM. She clearly enjoyed the company of celebrities. But she was much more comfortable among her Cracker and black friends, whose lives she honored and championed.

Thousands now visit her home at Cross Creek, which has recently been named a National Historic Landmark. She has been the subject of a U.S. commemorative stamp. Yet each time a new book on her is published, it must be accompanied by a spirited defense of who she was, what her contributions were, and why she is worthy of attention. Such defense is no longer required of her peers such as Eudora Welty, Flannery O'Connor, or Zora Neale Hurston. Why is it required of Rawlings? Why must she be defended before academe, which seems bent on considering her a regional writer lacking national stature and intellectual scope? One reason may be that these academics do not know that Rawlings herself defined and then rejected the paradoxical concept of "regional literature" as "not only false and unsound but dangerous" in an invited lecture before the National Council of English Teachers in 1939. Rawlings's fear was based upon her belief that the phrase would lead to the assumption that "if a piece of writing is regional, it is also literature." In drawing what for her is an essential distinction between regional literature and regional writing, Rawlings proclaims that "Ellen Glasgow stands alone in our generation as the creator of the only unmistakable regional literature of the South." She then discusses the work of Margaret Mitchell, Elizabeth Madox Roberts, and Zora Neale Hurston, whose *Moses, Man of the Mountain* (1939) "tempts me to admit her to my own private library of literature." She closes, ironically if not sarcastically, "There is perhaps question as to whether Faulkner is or is not a regional writer, but I should not so classify him. The storm-swept realm of the libido knows no geography."[1] Libidinous or not, if Faulkner or his reputation ever suffered from a "regional" classification, neither did so for very long. Glasgow and Hurston eventually joined Faulkner on the Olympus of universal literary acceptance, but only after a long critical negotiation. Mitchell and Roberts never did and never will find their way to such heights, but Rawlings should have long ago.

The plain truth is that Rawlings's historical presence, both as writer and as personality, should require no defense before the juries of academe. General readers devoted to her are increasing geometrically; those who do not fathom her stature, barely mathematically. The history of her ascendance in the 1930s and the 1940s, followed by her fall from grace thereafter, is common enough. Like most female writers of her generation, she achieved recognition, gathered acclaim, and then was tossed into the dustbin of the forgotten by an academic establishment oblivious of its own role in the perpetuation of male hegemony in literature. For nearly two decades, Rawlings was a giant in a male kingdom. At some juncture, not long after her death in 1953, her reputation as a writer of considerable import simply ceased to exist. To be sure, she was to some extent the victim of Time's Winged Chariot. Nothing new here. But in Rawlings's case she was also a victim of an academy determined to bury romantic sentiment in favor of coveted obscurity and cultural obfuscation. Nostalgia was eschewed; domesticity swept conveniently under the rug of oppression; race confined to the hypocritical smugness of scholarly self-defense. Thus, by the 1960s, if not a few years before, Rawlings had vanished from critical and intellectual sight in the gloaming of postmodern nescience.

We are still left with the question: Why? We could locate her demise under the rubric of gender bashing. She might have been tossed aside merely because of the secretive chauvinism of contemporary belles-lettres. Is it sufficient to argue that her novels—*The Yearling* was awarded the Pulitzer Prize for the Novel—lack innate qualities of "greatness," even though definition of those qualities has been and will forever be nebulously grounded in the ideologies of dominance? We are constantly reminded that "she is no Fitzgerald, no Hemingway, no Wolfe"? Must we say the obvious, that pedigree defined by gender is pedigree run amuck. It should be sufficient to point out that Perkins, the same editor of the aforementioned, storied triumvirate, thought Rawlings's second novel, *Golden Apples* (1935), the equal of Faulkner. It should be enough to establish that her first novel, *South Moon Under* (1933), gained immediate critical acclaim and was named as a finalist for the

Pulitzer Prize, or that her semi-autobiographical *Cross Creek* was hailed as an innovative, artistic triumph. And it should be enough to refer to the fact that for more than a decade she received accolades for the short fiction published in the major magazines of the day, such as *Scribner's*, the *New Yorker*, *Harper's*, and the *Saturday Evening Post*.

We would be remiss if we did not remember also that she walked in the most stellar of intellectual circles, so much so that she was considered a confidante by Perkins, who on separate occasions enlisted her to save Fitzgerald from the abyss of alcoholism, to encourage Hemingway to abandon his fatal propensity toward self-doubt, and to convince Wolfe to be less effusive in his prose. Fast forward. We might also mention that the celebrated contemporary novelist Pat Conroy listened as his mother read *The Yearling* (her favorite novel) to him as a boy, or that one of the brightest new literary lights, novelist Ron Rash, has identified *Cross Creek* as one of the five works that inspire his career. Nor is it meaningless that a cadre of women writers, from Doris Betts to Dorothy Allison to Barbara Kingsolver, has traveled a path that Rawlings helped to blaze. As Harper Lee recently commented, "Women writers like Marjorie Rawlings and my southern sisters, like Fannie Flagg, have cut a trail through the wilderness."[2] The examples of her fame and of her influence, here and abroad, are endless and, yes, nurturing to those willing to listen. Let us turn, then, to testimony by her contemporaries, specifically to Margaret Mitchell, who concluded that Rawlings was a "born perfect storyteller," or to Wallace Stevens, who thought Rawlings a "very remarkable woman."[3] Perhaps in the end it is not neces-

sary to defend her before the academy, for she defends herself
well enough.

The Biography

Just who then is this "born perfect storyteller," this "very remarkable woman"? As Lord Byron advises in *Don Juan*, let us
begin at the beginning.

Marjorie Kinnan was born in Washington, D.C., on 8 August 1896, the daughter of a successful examiner in the U.S.
Patent Office, who preferred wonder to fact, and of an officious,
somewhat overbearing mother, who preferred fact to wonder.
It is not surprising that the child Marjorie identified immediately with her father, who made certain that her education
included horseback riding and walking through the woods on
his Maryland dairy farm. Marjorie was precocious, at times
difficult. Her world was the world of the imagination. She was
forever making up stories and then telling them to her friends
on the doorsteps of her Washington home. She possessed an
inherent gift for gab, for invention, for wonder. Her imaginary
conversations soon took root. From 1910 to 1912, she became
a fixture on the Children's Page of the *Washington Post*, and in
1912, *McCall's Magazine* formally launched her literary career
by publishing her story "The Reincarnation of Miss Hetty,"
for which she was awarded second place in their fiction con-
test. Marjorie Kinnan never looked back. She edited her high
school magazine and contributed a number of stories to it, as
well as editorials and features to the school newspaper.[4] Kinnan, the imaginative artist, mingled easily with Kinnan, the

fact-oriented journalist. From these days of fictive experiment, she saw the necessity of controlling imaginative wonder with an essence of reportorial fact. Her teenage stories were deliberately moral in tone, seeking always to instruct. In 1914, she matriculated at the then celebrated "writer's school," the University of Wisconsin, but not before she had achieved a cornucopia of honors from Western High School in Washington, later renamed the Duke Ellington School for the Performing Arts.

When Marjorie Kinnan arrived at the University of Wisconsin in 1914, she was already credentialed and quickly made her presence known. She joined literary societies, she helped edit the yearbook, and she won awards for her thespian skills in various University-sponsored dramas, one written by her. However, all was not fun and games. War had broken out in Europe, and a number of students left the University to join the cause. Kinnan was patriotic to the core. She began to question University social functions that she felt improper in such dire times. As she watched the young men march away—women were forbidden to serve—she began to question her own elitist positions as her moral conscience convinced her that privilege was especially inappropriate in a time of war. She wore her conscience on her shoulder. She wrote editorials and open letters, some acerb, to the President of the University imploring him to address appropriately the dire circumstances.[5] Through it all, however, she managed to maintain her sense of self. She was, after all, a student, a profoundly gifted student, elected to Phi Beta Kappa in her junior year. She recognized the value of achievement and was graduated with honors in English in 1918.

After departing Madison, Rawlings was left for the first time to face the world on her own. As chance would have it, romance blossomed in spite of the mandates of patriotism. Her life was altered forever. In her senior year, she announced her engagement to Charles Rawlings Jr., a fellow student, whose handsome exterior and inviting personality had won her over. It did not hurt that, like her, he professed literature as his singular love. Charles Rawlings Jr. and Marjorie Kinnan were married in 1919, after she had followed him to New York, where he had been drafted into the military. Her love for him was unabashed, more teenager than adult. She wrote daily letters to him at his Brooklyn base, often filled with youthful mush. Yet they also contained accounts of Marjorie's trials and tribulations as she braved the pavements of New York City looking for publishers for her unpolished fiction. She managed to place only one story, but found multiple venues for her factual work, and in 1919 she published no fewer than seven feature articles, each displaying her developing penchant for women's issues.[6] Remarkable, really, for a young woman just graduated from college.

However, such work provided little sustenance, and less creative satisfaction. Desperate and without financial reserves, she worked part time for the YWCA, helping to edit training manuals. Stark reality had replaced the ideals of Wisconsin. Success, what the philosopher William James termed the "Bitch Goddess," was neither imminent nor forthcoming. Her ideals were challenged. Circumstances were difficult for her. Her life became one of foment, and her anger spilled out in letters to Charles. Cross, often threatening, the letters to him were followed immediately by abject apologies. To Charles, Marjorie confided her spirit, her feminist side. Fortunately, for both, Charles was mustered out of the army; unfortunately, for both, they now had to live together. The feminist Marjorie and the chauvinist Charles were explosively mismatched, even though there were a number of temporary hiatuses. She lived with Charles's parents in Rochester for a time, while he traveled the Midwest as a salesman, eventually a confused, failed salesman, not unlike Willy Loman. Like Marjorie, he wanted more; he wanted the glory of authorship. In 1920, they moved to Louisville, Kentucky, to follow their dreams. Marjorie was fortunate enough to land a job as a feature writer for the *Louisville Courier-Journal*, writing the always feminist, always moral column "Live Women in Live Louisville."[7] She had a propensity for the journalistic—that is, for capturing a moment by displaying restraint. Similar to Hemingway at the *Kansas City Star*, she used newspaper work as the training ground for a life as a creative writer.

As Marjorie moved inexorably forward, Charles slipped slowly, painfully backward. In addition to her newspaper work, Marjorie was able to publish a few nondescript stories and features.[8] The pressure on Charles to live up to her expectations and talents became enormous. With neither the talent nor the diligence necessary to enable genius, he began to founder. To save their marriage, they returned to upstate New York in 1921, where she became a feature writer for Rochester newspapers, and in 1923, she wrote a satiric column for the popular society rag *Five O'Clock*, under the nom de plume "Lady Alicia Thwaite."[9] In May 1926, she began to write a series of poems for the *Rochester Times-Union* under the rubric "Songs of a Housewife."[10] By the time this syndicated column ended in February 1928, she had written and published, daily, 495 poems. The poems are not stellar—hack work, really—but they do display a developing wit melding with her feminist sensibility. More important, they reveal a writer working hard at being a writer. Charles continued to fall farther behind. Desperation ensued. Their marriage teetered on the rocks of dissolution. To save themselves from themselves, they made what appeared to be an incredibly misguided decision, a move to Florida.

In 1928, shortly after she completed an autobiographical novel, *Blood of My Blood*, what she called "poor Jane Austen," largely about her mother, the Rawlingses decided to use their very last dollars to buy a seventy-two-acre orange grove, which just happened to be located in the most remote, almost aboriginal, hammocks of north central Florida. They, in effect, decided to abandon the creature comforts of the North for the critter comforts of the tiny hamlet of Cross Creek. The now not so young romantics settled among potentially injurious wildlife and mostly irascible Cracker neighbors in order to fulfill the utopian ideal of devoting their lives to writing. Such devotion came at a high price. Marjorie, after much trial and error, adapted; Charles, with little effort at trial much less error, failed. Epical battles ensued, some physical. Charles fled to the relative safety of Tampa, wrote a few articles with nautical themes, and finally returned to the North. The always mismatched couple was divorced in November 1933.

Cross Creek became almost immediately a source of inspiration for Rawlings. She began as a Yankee, according to her Cracker neighbors, even though she always insisted that her Maryland heritage made her a daughter of the South if not of the Confederacy. Her reputation quickly grew among the denizens of the Creek. Like them, she lived off the land. She fed off the luminous stories told to her by her Cracker friends and black neighbors, many of whom adopted her first out of curiosity, then respect, and finally love. Her presence transformed them, but more important, their presence transformed her. She learned the customs and the language of the Crackers, who lived lives of quiet desperation, locked in a poverty tempered by a curious rustic nobility. She trained herself in Cracker lore. The stories they told her and the language they provided her became the fodder for her work, as did the folktales, often supernatural, related to her by her black workers, whom she particularly grew to admire and to love. Rawlings not only found a sense of place at Cross Creek; she also found her voice, her muse.

In the spring of 1930, with requisite trepidation, she sent off a cluster of stories about Cracker life to Charles Scribner's Sons with the impossible hope that the publisher might even care to reply. To her shock, back came, almost at once, a letter from Maxwell E. Perkins, whose attention fledgling writers merely dreamed of, much less received. Without reserve, Perkins encouraged her, suggesting how she might improve this story with metaphor and that story with language. The result was her first major publication, a group of stories given the title "Cracker Chidlings," which was published in *Scribner's Magazine* in 1931 and followed by a novella, "Jacob's Ladder," about a young Cracker bride who must learn to survive in a male world. Then came the stunningly feminist story about a psychologically abused woman who achieves dignity through marital encounter, "Gal Young Un" (1932), which in 1933 won the O. Henry Award, first prize, for the best short story of the year. Perkins, through no fault of his own, lost this prize-winning story to *Harper's*, a mistake that never occurred again at Scribners.

Emboldened by such success, Rawlings then sent a full-length manuscript about the romantically brutal essence of Cracker culture to Perkins, who took it with unbridled enthusiasm. After some hands-on direction from Perkins on how to improve the manuscript, it was published under the intriguing title *South Moon Under* (1933) to immediate critical acclaim. But more important for Scribners and for Rawlings, the novel sold widely, more than 46,000 copies inclusive of the Book-of-the-Month Club printings.[11] For the first time in her career, Rawlings had some spare cash to spend. She used it, among other things, to repair her roof and to install an indoor toilet. However, the joys of authorship, as always, came with a price. The effusive Rawlings became more effusive. Words were her panacea; food and liquor her companions. She wrote and partied with abandon. She was an expert cook and an expert host, a reputation not overlooked by her friend, become companion, become lover, Norton S. Baskin, hotelier and raconteur, whose rural Alabama upbringing provided Rawlings with yet another source of inspiration. After a lengthy, often volatile, on-again, off-again courtship, they were finally married in October 1941.

During it all, the excitement of love and of authorship, Rawlings persisted in her work. A number of her short fiction pieces gained recognition, but nothing and no one could defuse her determination to write a novel about an Englishman who came to Florida to grow citrus. Perkins cautioned against the theme, believing that she was abandoning the simplicity of her Cracker base for a complex psychological novel outside her ken. She did not heed Perkins's advice. Her stubborn persistence became almost mania. And in the end *Golden Apples* (1935) issued forth to little fanfare. It simply did not generate the critical enthusiasm that had welcomed *South Moon Under*. Sales were modest, 15,000 copies through two printings.[12]

Perkins felt compelled to guide Rawlings back to her roots, and urged her to write a "boy's book" about the dignity of Cracker life. Rawlings resisted. There followed again much trial and plenty of error. But under the guidance of Perkins, who suggested both metaphor and plot, and even came up with the title, Rawlings completed the manuscript, with no expectation whatsoever that the book would achieve any success. She was, in fact, depressed by her effort to write about a Cracker boy who gains maturation only after he is forced to shoot his pet fawn. Once again, Rawlings was mistaken. Her "boy's book," with the Perkins-suggested title *The Yearling*, gained instant praise and fame. It remained on the best-seller list for twenty-three consecutive weeks, and in the first year went through sixteen printings, selling in excess of 240,000 copies, a number that does not include Book-of-the-Month Club sales of more than 108,000. The film rights sold to MGM brought an astonishing $30,000.[13] But more important, the novel was awarded the Pulitzer Prize for the Novel in 1939. Rawlings was now an international superstar. Not surprisingly, both she and Scribners reaped huge benefits.

But as the poet Keats reminds us in "Sleep and Poetry," fame does not come easily, and its laurel is worn with difficulty. The joy of success took from her the relative anonymity Cross Creek had provided for nearly a decade. Celebrity confronted and confounded her. Newspapers, universities, women's clubs, devoted fans, each and all besieged her. She went on the lecture circuit. The accolades kept coming. In an attempt to find escape from both fame and the brutal inland heat, she bought a cottage at Crescent Beach, only to be beleaguered further by fans and friends. Such distractions, although enjoyable, even profitable, caused the muse to slip and her health to suffer. Too much food and too much revelry ground at her creative soul and played havoc with her body. She needed silence. She got little. Through it all, Norton Baskin was her rock. He guided her, he made her laugh, and in the end he loved her without reservation. Perkins also hovered protectively. He let her have her space, while at the same time kept her career in balance. In 1940, Scribners published her next book, *When the Whippoor-will*—, a collection of previously published short stories as well as excerpts from her novels. Such books sell, and they do keep the writer's name before the public, but they do little to fulfill the creative spirit. Incredibly, Rawlings somehow managed to get back to work. She revisited partly completed manuscript stories about her life at Cross Creek, which she had begun years before. She wanted to write a semi-factual, semi-creative, semi-autobiographical narrative, not an easy task to accomplish, for genres inevitably compete against one another. Perkins was fully supportive and read endless start-ups that she sent him.

The result once again catapulted her to the top of her profession. *Cross Creek* (1942), a series of loosely connected vignettes, became an instant best seller. Nearly 500,000 copies were printed, inclusive of the Book-of-the-Month Club, in the first year of publication.[14] *Cross Creek* might be described as an ebbing and flowing confluence of reality and fiction, for in it Rawlings successfully marries fact with wonder. Her journalistic instinct to report was carefully united with her fictive instinct to create. Her celebrity was renewed. Scribners immediately followed with *Cross Creek Cookery* (1942), a cookbook of favorite recipes laced with interlinear commentary. Rawlings enjoyed considerable remuneration, although it meant far less to her than recognition. But, as always, she was to pay a price. A local neighbor, whom she attempted to describe wittily and honestly in *Cross Creek* as an "ageless spinster resembling an angry and efficient canary,"[15] took exception to the hurtful portrayal and filed a lawsuit for libel, later changed to "invasion of privacy." The trial created a sensation, gained national attention, and lingered on for years. Rawlings was eventually found innocent by a jury of her peers, but upon appeal, the Florida Supreme Court found her guilty and fined her one dollar, plus court costs.[16]

The so-called Cross Creek Trial, an adventure in theater and theatrics while at the same time a landmark interrogation of personal and artistic rights, was not Rawlings's only tribulation. In 1943, as the trial was getting under way, her beloved

Norton suddenly enlisted in the Ambulance Field Service and was assigned to the India/Burma campaign, where he quickly contracted malaria and began to waste away. Marjorie was beside herself. She wrote letters of appeal to get him sent home, and in the end she was successful. The once dapper Norton arrived home emaciated, for a time near death, and it took him (and her) years to recover. The strain on Rawlings was overwhelming. She could get little of a literary nature done. All of this stress was exacerbated by her determination to answer fully each and every letter she received from service people, many of whom were going into battle, some of whom did not survive. These young people (she had not forgotten those students at the University of Wisconsin who also had marched off to war) were, to her, children once removed. She advised them on all manner of issues, not the least of which was how to confront the possibility of death.

To cope with the trial, Norton's near fatal experience, and the fear and love expressed to her by the service people, Marjorie escaped as best she could, often with liquor and food. Again her muse suffered. The manuscript of what eventually became *The Sojourner*, finally published in 1953, was mired in ennui. She bought a home in Van Hornesville, New York, to attempt revival. The manuscript was worked over, and worked over, and worked over, and then revised. Even the proximity of her close friend Robert Frost offered little solace. As from the beginning of her career, her dogged persistence paid off, but not until after the unexpected death of her treasured friend and invaluable mentor Maxwell Perkins in 1947, an event from which she never fully recovered. The transcendental-pulsed *The Sojourner*, based upon the histories of her ancestors in Michigan, lacks the flame of spirit that enlivens *The Yearling* and *Cross Creek*. Although not dull, neither is it inspired. It was met with mixed reviews and modest sales, just under 50,000 copies.[17]

Rawlings's plaintive muse was quietly, inexorably going to sleep. She died suddenly, although not unexpectedly, on 13 December 1953, at Flagler Hospital in St. Augustine. She was fifty-seven. The medics said she had suffered a ruptured aneurysm. But those who knew her well knew better. She died too exhausted to live another day. She could no longer resist what her friend Dylan Thomas called "that good night." She is buried at Antioch Cemetery, appropriately located among sand roads and endless hammocks, near Island Grove, Florida. As John Cardinal Newman sings, she was only "lost awhile" to Norton. Ever her beloved courtier, Norton died in 1997 at the age of ninety-five. He now rests beside her. Marjorie's love for Norton was never qualified, and is expressed cherishingly in a letter she wrote to Ellen Glasgow: Norton is "so generous, so tolerant and so tender, and we care for each other in so deep and quiet a way, that being with him is like coming home into harbor after a long storm."[18] Reflecting his ever-present humility, Norton had inscribed on her gravestone:

MARJORIE KINNAN RAWLINGS
1896–1953
wife of
NORTON BASKIN
THROUGH HER WRITINGS SHE ENDEARED
HERSELF TO THE PEOPLE OF THE WORLD

No better words need be sought. Rawlings lived life to the lees. Readers everywhere are the richer for it.

The Text

Choosing passages as representative of Rawlings's canon has been difficult, indeed. There is such a wealth of material. To provide some scope and control, we have selected passages only from her novels and from her short fiction from the Florida Period (1928–1953). There is a wealth of other material in her pre-Florida short fiction, her letters, and her essays. But space would not permit us to go too far afield. Choice also betrays the prejudices of the choosers. There is no doubt that we as editors have omitted passages that are favorites of other readers. How could it be otherwise, so rich, so ravishing, so eternal are Rawlings's words. What we set out to do was to capture essence, to reproduce those passages that we felt to be representative of the majesty of Rawlings's immense talent of using evocative language, of provoking metaphor, and of inspiring description. We have also tried to achieve some balance in the quotations, although it should not be surprising that *The Yearling* and *Cross Creek* dominate. They are, after all, Rawlings's consummate literary achievements. Still, we attempted to be representative, to combine the flavor of the maturing Rawlings with that of the matured Rawlings. In the end, our most difficult task was placing the quotations into categories. Such thematic placement works against the universality Rawlings herself professed. That is, a quotation might appear to be, let us say, about Autumn, but in fact is a universal expression of eternity. Or, a reader might find a quotation in a section called Earth that might just as easily deserve inclusion under the rubric of Time, or Place, or Stewardship. We have differentiated these passages into categories while acknowledging the many contradictions and limitations inherent in the very concept of category. In response to this difficulty, we have drawn on the elements of the ancient Greeks and on the immortal seasons as well as on Rawlings's language to create a kind of unifying foundation, upon which we have created arbitrary groupings such as "Place," "Creeturs," "Flora," and "Human Nature."

The texts for the quotations are from the first editions, unless otherwise noted. Research has found that Rawlings changed little of a substantive nature as her texts went through various printings and iterations. There are exceptions. For example, in the School Book Edition of *The Yearling*, she edited out certain racist language that she left in the trade edition. Since we used first editions for our quotations, accounting for minor textual changes in other editions was not an issue. Because there are so many quotations, we had to adopt the strategy of using ellipses to indicate dropped language and/or excised paragraphs. Since this is a volume devoted to the very best of Rawlings, we thought this strategy superior to inclusivity at the risk of exclusivity. However, we attempted always to be prudent when it came to the dropping of language from a passage.

Finally, it should be noted that this is a book of quotations, designed to inspire and to edify. It is not a scholarly tome where primary text is subordinated to critical inquiry. This is Rawlings's book, not the editors'. The language is hers. We have not intruded with notes of explanation or opinions on meaning. This book is meant to be read as a cornucopia of Rawlings's unparalleled ability to transform language into metaphor and metaphor into meaning. One need not read it from beginning to end. It can be dipped into without fear of loss. It is what the Victorians referred to as a "parlor book," one to be kept out and to be consulted at leisure. In *Cross Creek*, Rawlings describes "one's own minute living" as "a torn fragment of the larger cloth."[19] We send forth our selection of fragments from the larger cloth of Rawlings's genius, knowing that as fragments they metonymically reveal that genius in its entirety. We wish all readers the best of experiences, as you are challenged, delighted, and instructed by an artist of unquestionable renown and eternal verity.

Notes

1. "Regional Literature of the South," in *Uncollected Writings*, by Rawlings, 272–73, 277–79; see also *College English* 1, no. 1 (February 1940): 381–89.

2. See Marcia Lane, "Rawlings Group Gathers," *St. Augustine Record*, 15 April 2010.

3. Tarr, introduction to *Short Stories by Marjorie Kinnan Rawlings*, 25.

4. See Tarr, *Descriptive Bibliography*, 179–83; and Rawlings, *Uncollected Writings*, 15–71.

5. See Tarr, *Descriptive Bibliography*, 183–87; and Rawlings, *Uncollected Writings*, 88–152.

6. See Tarr, *Descriptive Bibliography*, 187–88; and Rawlings, *Uncollected Writings*, 154–82.

7. See Tarr, *Descriptive Bibliography*, 187–88; and Rawlings, *Uncollected Writings*, 186–208.

8. See Tarr, *Descriptive Bibliography*, 188; and Rawlings, *Uncollected Writings*, 209–14.

9. See Tarr, *Descriptive Bibliography*, 189–90; and Rawlings, *Uncollected Writings*, 233–44.

10. See Tarr, *Descriptive Bibliography*, 190–227; and Rawlings, *Songs of a Housewife*.

11. See Tarr, *Descriptive Bibliography*, 7.

12. See Tarr, *Descriptive Bibliography*, 26–28.

13. See Tarr, *Descriptive Bibliography*, 38–39.

14. See Tarr, *Descriptive Bibliography*, 99.

15. Rawlings, *Cross Creek*, 48.

16. For a complete account of the trail and its aftermath, see Acton, *Invasion of Privacy*.

17. See Tarr, *Descriptive Bibliography*, 133–34.

18. Rawlings to Glasgow, 17 January 1942, in Rawlings, *Selected Letters*, 216. At her death, Rawlings was well into compiling materials for a biography of Ellen Glasgow, a biography that would have revealed explosive facts about Glasgow's personal life. The loss of this biography—a writer reflecting on another writer and a close friend—is incalculable.

19. Rawlings, *Cross Creek*, 39.

Marjorie Kinnan Rawlings's Cross Creek Sampler

Earth

Rawlings's Cross Creek house as seen from the orange grove, 1950s. Courtesy of the Department of Special and Area Studies Collections, George A. Smathers Libraries, University of Florida.

For we are strangers before thee, and sojourners, as were all our fathers: our days on the earth are as a shadow, and there is none abiding.

1 Chronicles 29:15; epigraph of *The Sojourner*

Folk call the road lonely, because there is not human traffic and human stirring. Because I have walked it so many times and seen such a tumult of life there, it seems to me one of the most populous highways of my acquaintance. I have walked it in ecstasy, and in joy it is beloved. Every pine tree, every gallberry bush, every passion vine, every joree rustling in the underbrush, is vibrant. I have walked it in trouble, and the wind in the trees beside me is easing. I have walked it in despair, and the red of the sunset is my own blood dissolving into the night's darkness. For all such things were on earth before us, and will survive after us, and it is given to us to join ourselves with them and to be comforted.

Cross Creek, 6

Jody pondered the strangeness of it. The creatures of the water and the creatures of the air had survived. Only things whose home was the solid land itself, had perished, trapped between the alien elements of wind and water. The thought was one of those that stirred him, and that he could never bring to earth to share with his father. It moved now across his mind like a remnant of the morning's haze.

The Yearling, 304

The evening was clear and rosy. The sun was drawing water. Shadowy fingers reached through the luminous sky to the sodden earth.

The Yearling, 249

On the way home he considered the deer and the moon. He considered the fish and the owls. The deer and the rabbits, the fish and the owls, stirred at moon-rise and at moon-down; at south-moon-over and at south-moon-under. The moon swung around the earth, or the earth swung around the moon, he was not sure. The moon rose in the east and that was moon-rise. Six hours later it hung at its zenith between east and west, and that was south-moon-over. It set in the west and that was moon-down. Then it passed from sight and swung under the earth, between west and east. And when it was directly under the earth, that was south-moon-under.

South Moon Under, 109

I stared at his hands. They were the hands of a black father, cradling the helpless children of the earth.

"In the Heart," *Short Stories,* 319

As long as the whole continued, the earth could go about its business. And if the sun's work was one day done and the earth cooled to desolation and all its folk and foliage with it, somewhere on or in or among other suns and earths and stars, the life pulse would continue, indestructible, eternal, the Life to which men gave the name of God. Of this he was certain.

The Sojourner, 143

He marvelled, padding on bare feet past the slat-fence of the clearing, that the moon was so strong that when it lay on the other side of the earth, the creatures felt it and stirred by the hour it struck. The moon was far away, unseen, and it had power to move them.

South Moon Under, 110

Neither river nor swamp nor hammock nor impenetrable scrub could save a man from the ultimate interference. There was no safety. There was no retreat. Forces beyond his control, beyond his sight and hearing, took him in their vast senseless hands when they were ready. The whole earth must move as the sun and moon and an obscure law directed—even the earth, planet-ridden and tormented.

South Moon Under, 327

He went to work intently. . . . The flutter-mill was at work. . . . Up, over, down, up, over, down—the flutter-mill was enchanting. The bubbling spring would rise forever from the earth, the thin current was endless. The spring was the beginning of waters sliding to the sea. Unless leaves fell, or squirrels cut sweet bay twigs to drop and block the fragile wheel, the flutter-mill might turn forever.

The Yearling, 5–6

A small world lay at his feet. It was deep and concave, like a great bowl. Fodder-wing said that a bear as big as God had scooped out a pawful of earth to get a lily-root. Jody knew the truth from his father. It was only that underground rivers ran through the earth and swirled and eddied beneath the surface, and changed their courses.

The Yearling, 79

"They ain't no good in it. Lest it is to remind a man to be humble, for there's nary thing on earth he kin call his own."

Penny on seven days of rain, *The Yearling*, 236

Without Penny, there was no comfort anywhere. The solid earth had dissolved under him. His bitterness absorbed his sorrow, and they were one. . . . A fresh wave of loneliness swept over him. He had lost Flag and he had lost his father, too.

The Yearling, 415–16

He felt surely, but humbly, too, conscious of his ignorance, that horror was abroad on the earth, and had asked himself what any one man might do to stop it. He could not be alone, or simple-minded, in considering war too primitive an attempt to resolve the differences among men's varying greeds, among their differences of mind and philosophy.

The Sojourner, 302

The sink-hole lay all in shadow. Suddenly it seemed to Jody that Fodder-wing had only now gone away with the raccoons. Something of him had been always where

the wild creatures fed and played. Something of him would be always near them. Fodder-wing was like the trees. He was of the earth, as they were earthy, with his gnarled, frail roots deep in the sand.

The Yearling, 219

Nothing could harm Penny for long. Not even a rattlesnake, he thought comfortingly, could kill him. Penny was inviolable, as the earth was inviolable.

The Yearling, 392

The full moon was quieting the earth's upheaval, was smoothing the fields, the pastures, the now dark farmhouses, the small towns through which the train was passing with sad sweet whistle blowing. He saw the moon itself. The railroad tracks must have taken a turn, so to bring the moon into view. The steady pound of the train was soothing. He fell deep asleep.

The Sojourner, 312

He decided that the sunrise and sunset both gave him a pleasant sad feeling. The sunrise brought a wild, free sadness; the sunset, a lonely yet a comforting one. He indulged his agreeable melancholy until the earth under him turned from gray to lavender and then to the color of dried corn husks. He went at his work vigorously.

The Yearling, 397

He saw the earth plainly as a battered planet. The skin was cracked and wrinkled, gashed with canyons, torn and split by rivers. Mountains were jumbles of sterile stone. Cities were already ruins, as though he saw them a thousand years in the future, or in the past. Only the farms and fields were beautiful. Green and red and golden and violet squares and rectangles spoke of man's sole kindness to the earth.

The Sojourner, 325

I thought of the countless generations that had "owned" land. Of what did that ownership consist? I thought of the great earth, whirling in space. It was here ahead of men and could conceivably be here after them. How should one man say that he "owned" any piece or parcel of it? If he worked with it, labored to bring it to fruition, it seemed to me that at most he held it in fief.

Cross Creek, 367

Stewardship

A man was a puny thing, frightened and lonely; transitory and unimportant. When he blended himself with whatever was greater than he, he found peace. He shared the importance of growth and continuity. When a man shaped growth to his ends, he put his hand on the secret core of creation, and in the shaping was a moment's mastery, and in the mastery was his dignity. He joined himself to the earth, and because the earth itself was a little part of a farther universe, he joined himself through it to the stars, and in the union was his ecstasy.

Golden Apples, 351

Jody cast and cast again, but there was never the mad swirl in the waters. . . . He caught a small bass and held it up to show his father. "Throw him back," Penny called. "We don't need him for eatin'. Leave him to grow up big as t'other one. Then we'll come back agin and ketch him." Jody put the small fish back reluctantly and watched it swim away. His father was stern about not taking more of anything, fish or game, than could be eaten or kept.

The Yearling, 93–94

The entire region was again almost a virgin wilderness. Yet the law had come into the scrub and lay over it like a dark cloud. Several years ago the government had taken over the greater bulk of it, unowned, uninhabited. Thousands of acres at its heart were now a game refuge, where no one might hunt or trap. Fire towers had been established here and there. There had been panic among the few inhabitants.

South Moon Under, 233

I began my hunting there, practicing with a .410 on the gray squirrels that whisked up and down the tree trunks. There was great sport at first in all the hunting. Then it came to sicken me, and now I go to the pines as a guest and not an invader.

Cross Creek, 36

She had shared in history, and she would tell her class on Monday that they had shared, too. And she would tell them—oh, she would tell them again and again—that the battle was not yet won, that one human being must be kind to another, one race, one nation to another, or the world was lost.

"Miss Moffatt Steps Out," *Short Stories*, 367

Birds and small furred creatures cowered in the shadow of hawk and owl. But the clearing was safe. Penny kept it so, with his good fences.

The Yearling, 142

My heart bursts with the loveliness of the grove and of the night. If only, I think, I could watch such beauty unencumbered by my fears. Then I know that a part of the beauty is the fight to keep it, and that all good things do not come easily and must perpetually be fought for. Our test is in our recognition of our love and our willingness to do battle for it. Sometimes the battle is hopeless.

Cross Creek, 336

The season was the May of this year. I withdrew into the turtle shell of my mortality. It was good to know there would be pecans, unexpectedly, this November. I turned away and left them to their maturing.

Cross Creek, 244

"It's really not so frightful to shoot them, . . . for if a covey isn't shot into and broken up, it stays together and the quail don't mate that year."

MKR to Aunt Wilmer, *Cross Creek*, 320

Game birds have an added flavor when you have shot them yourself, or have at least been on the shoot. I am a poor shot, and hypocritically have little true desire to do better. What makes the sport is the magnificent country and the stirring performance of good dogs. Good companions lift it into high adventure, and while there are solitary souls who rove the fields alone with dog and gun, it is one of the pastimes that I, who can do with much solitude and like to walk alone, prefer to share. But the birds I have downed would not make a respectable covey. Some day I shall lay down my arms entirely.

Cross Creek, 319

My profane friend Zelma, the census taker, said, "The b——s killed the egrets for their plumage until the egrets gave out. They killed alligators for their hides until the alligators gave out. If the frogs ever give out, the sons of b——s will starve to death."

Cross Creek, 147

Life and Death

Rawlings and one of her favorite hunting companions, Norton S. Baskin. Courtesy of the Department of Special and Area Studies Collections, George A. Smathers Libraries, University of Florida.

All life is a balance, when it is not a battle, between the forces of creation and the forces of destruction, between love and hate, between life and death. Perhaps it is impossible ever to say where one ends and the other begins, for even creation and destruction are relative. This morning I crushed a fuzzy black caterpillar.

Cross Creek, 364

But in crushing the caterpillar, I have fed the ants. They are hustling to the feast, already tunnelling the body. The ants would applaud the treading of caterpillars. The death of a human feeds, apparently, nothing. Or are there psychic things that are nourished by our annihilation?

Cross Creek, 364–365

Seems like we could of got borned without so much meanness in us.

Quincey Dover, "Cocks Must Crow," *Short Stories*, 252

The heifer was indeed in trouble. The calf was large and the heifer young. He was obliged to help, to pull the wet thing into the world. The heifer went at once to the devouring of the afterbirth. He was familiar with this apparent monstrosity and it had always puzzled him. Yet somehow it made all of life an endless cycle. There was first of all the love, and he was certain the animals felt love as well as humans, for no female of horse or dog or kine could be forced to accept a male unwillingly. So the male element permeated the female, the seed lay deep, as the seeds in the earth, there was the long gestation, the release then, and the triumph of birth and of harvest. Perhaps the bovine swallowing of the after-birth was only another step in the eternal nourishment, beginning the great round once again.

The Sojourner, 75

In the sustaining of life were pain and pleasure. Her mother had only understood the pain.

South Moon Under, 41

The words were like a bone thrown to a good dog by the fire. He felt lost, almost an outsider. The world had turned completely female. He seemed to have had nothing to do with the child, nothing with the woman. He was only tolerated in his own house. The she-rites of fertility possessed it. He heard then the wail, the strange, anguished, angry protest against human birth.

The Sojourner, 60

Fodder-wing seemed made of tallow, like a candle. Suddenly he was familiar. Jody whispered, "Hey."

The Yearling, 203

In the breeding season, from late fall through winter and spring, until June or July, the drakes infuriate me so that I swear I shall eat them all. Their love life is merciless, public and continuous. The chickens mate so casually, a mere duty to be done, that the onlooker thinks nothing of it. The drakes are Rabelaisian, they are Turks, they are Huns. The ducks go for months with pecked heads and lamed legs.

Cross Creek, 254

"I don't like no female stock around, no-ways. Mules ain't bad that-a-way, because a mule don't know to do wrong. But the time I been havin' with my ol' cow— broke thu the fence last night and gone yonder to Sellers's bull. I jest don't want no female thing around the place."

"You'll have a devil of a time gittin' milk from ary thing else."

Raynes and Luke, *Golden Apples*, 332

Taking in a local square dance as a spectator she had met a young Cracker and fallen absurdly in love with him, for the mating instinct knows no classes.

Cross Creek, 53

She drew back the bed covers for him. There were lace and blue ribbons at the throat of her night-dress. Her eyes were bright in the firelight. Her breathing was fast. He was trembling but there was no uncertainty in his strong arms and limbs. She met him avidly. The miracle mounted on pulsing wings, soared over spaceless peaks and throbbed away into the distance with silver feathers fluttering.

The Sojourner, 44–45

The bee violated the bloom, the redbird violated his mate, the dog violated the bitch, and the thing was done with ecstasy, for the inscrutable purposes of creation. It was absurd that among men and women, the good should harm.

Golden Apples, 207–8

"I'll be dogged if I see how you women-folks figure the moon when it comes to birthin' young uns. Don't none of you go that high to get one."

Lorimer, *South Moon Under*, 58

But just as sure as cooters crawls before a rain, why, we got no right to holler about such things as getting old and dying.

Quincey Dover, "Cocks Must Crow," *Short Stories*, 252

The rain on his clean skin made him feel clean and free. The lightning flashed and he was startled by his own whiteness. He felt suddenly defenceless. He was lone and naked in an unfriendly world; lost and forgotten in the storm and darkness. Something ran behind him and ahead of him. It stalked the scrub like a panther. It was vast and formless and it was his enemy. Ol' Death was loose in the scrub.

The Yearling, 153

Out in the scrub, the war waged ceaselessly. The bears and wolves and panthers and wild-cats all preyed on the deer. Bears even ate cubs of other bears, all meat being to their maws the same. Squirrels and wood-rats, 'possums and 'coons, must all scurry for their lives.

The Yearling, 142

"When one man's on-reasonable, t'other has got to keep his head. I ain't big enough to fight him jest-so. All I could of done was to of takened the gun and shot him. When I kill a man, hit'll be for somethin' more serious than a ignorant man's meanness."

Penny, *The Yearling*, 310–11

Now he understood. This was death. Death was a silence that gave back no answer. Fodder-wing would never speak to him again.

The Yearling, 203–4

"Well, hit's a stone wall nobody's yit clumb over. You kin kick it and crack your head agin it and holler, but nobody'll listen and nobody'll answer."

Penny on death, *The Yearling*, 248–49

The sheriff shot and Marsh fell and it was the end of glamor at Cross Creek.

Cross Creek, 143

"Leave off! Ain't it enough to have trouble with the animals without the family quarrelin'? Has a man got to die to find peace?"

Penny, *The Yearling*, 288

"He'll grow a good bit bigger. He'll be betwixt and between. He'll be like a person standin' on the state line. He'll be leavin' one and turnin into t'other. Behind him's the fawn. Before him's the buck."

Penny, *The Yearling*, 380

"You're a pair o' yearlin's. . . . Hit grieves me."

Penny, The Yearling, 387

"Jody, all's been done was possible. I'm sorry. I cain't never tell you, how sorry. But we cain't have our year's crops destroyed, We cain't all go hungry. Take the yearlin' out in the woods and tie him and shoot him."

Penny, The Yearling, 402

"Hit's me! Hit's me! Flag!" . . . Flag lay beside the pool. He opened great liquid eyes and turned them on the boy with a glazed look of wonder. Jody pressed the muzzle of the gun barrel at the back of the smooth neck and pulled the trigger. Flag quivered a moment and then lay still.

The Yearling, 410

He had not yet probed the deepest pain. . . . "Pa went back on me." It was a sharper horror than if Penny had died of the snakebite. He rubbed his knuckles over his forehead. Death could be borne. Fodder-wing had died and he was able to bear it. Betrayal was intolerable.

Jody, The Yearling, 415

"You figgered I went back on you. Now there's a thing ever' man has got to know. Mebbe you know it a'ready. 'Twa'n't only me. 'Twa'n't only your yearlin' deer havin' to be destroyed. Boy, life goes back on you."

Penny, The Yearling, 426

"I've wanted life to be easy for you. Easier'n 'twas for
me. A man's heart aches, seein' his young uns face the
world. Knownin' they got to git their guts tore out, the
way his was tore. I wanted to spare you, long as I could.
I wanted you to frolic with your yearlin'. I knowed the
lonesomeness he eased for you. But ever' man's lonesome. What's he to do then? What's he to do when
he gits knocked down? Why, take it for his share and
go on."

Penny, The Yearling, 426

"You've done come back different. You've takened a
punishment. You ain't a yearlin' no longer, Jody——"

Penny, The Yearling, 426

In the beginning of his sleep, he cried out, "Flag!" It
was not his own voice that called. It was a boy's voice.
Somewhere beyond the sink-hole, past the magnolia,
under the live oaks, a boy and a yearling ran side by
side, and were gone forever.

The Yearling, 428

Many a hardened hunter has told me that he is done
with his deer killing. When a clean kill is made, he
takes pleasure in the sport, but when the fallen deer is
yet alive when he comes up to it, and he must cut its
throat, he cannot face the big eyes turned on him with
a stricken wonder.

Cross Creek, 237

"I wouldn't be caught dead without a frill on me. Men-folks like a woman dressed pretty."

Grandma Hutto, *The Yearling*, 323

"I was raised to call it indecent, to dress to please the men. Well, some of us plain folks has had to go pore on this earth, 'll git our frills in Heaven."

Ma, *The Yearling*, 323

The balance of nature is a mysterious thing, and man must fight on one side or the other with caution, or he will find that in his battle he has exterminated some friendly element.

Cross Creek, 152

Only Mary huddled behind his chair with a desperate small face. Only she and I have missed him, finding the world less generous for his going.

On the death of Moe Sykes, *Cross Creek*, 121

It had been so brief a sojourn, not even a full century. He had been a guest in a mansion and he was not ungrateful. He was at once exhausted and refreshed. His stay was ended. Now he must gather up the shabby impedimenta of his mind and body and be on his way again.

The Sojourner, 327

4

· · · · · ·

Sowing and Reaping

Nothing was more important than growth. A man favored with the possession of land might choose what things he would grow; might make room for them to suit his will. He could not see how a man could ask more of living than to choose his crops and to command them; to merge himself with the earth; to follow the seasons and let the sun and rain unite the sweat of his body with the soil he tended; to dream in the long nights of shining groves and golden oranges.

Golden Apples, 74

It was savage and beautiful, with such treacheries as the freeze sheathed within it. It responded with passion to the stimulation of its cultivating. Yet man here was never quite the master.

Golden Apples, 282

"When the whip-poor-will calls, it's time for the corn to be in the ground."

Drenna, "A Crop of Beans," *Short Stories*, 143

Penny Baxter . . . was always wakeful on the full moon. He had often wondered whether, with the light so bright, men were not meant to go into the fields and labor.

The Yearling, 16

A day and a half completed the potato planting. A good night rain soaked the earth. Green sprouts appeared within a week, then crinkled leaves. The bean blossoms dried, the young beans were infinitesimal pointed swords. Sun and rain alternated, the beans matured rapidly. The winter wheat was ripening. Any breath of wind made it ripple like tawny flowing hair.

The Sojourner, 128

He cut into the sand road and began to run east. It was two miles to the Glen, but it seemed to Jody that he could run forever. There was no ache in his legs, as when he hoed the corn. He slowed down to make the road last longer. He had passed the big pines and left them behind. Where he walked now, the scrub had closed in, walling in the road with dense pines, each one so thin it seemed to the boy it might make kindling by itself.

The Yearling, 3

"Wind and rain got you beat down. . . . How they 'spect you to grow up, dirt and weeds 'round yo' necks? Lemme turn you loose—."

Bat to his marigolds, "In the Heart," *Short Stories,* 319

The afternoon was warm. . . . In a way, Jody thought, fishing was better than hunting. It was not so exciting, but neither was there terror. The heart beat at a reasonable cadence. There was time to look about, and see the increase of green leaves in the live oaks and magnolias.

The Yearling, 90

"Now that's the way to live. . . . All the good things we got here in Florida, blueberries and blackberries and beans and cow-peas, all them things had ought to be canned and put up on a clean cupboard shelf with white paper on it. That's the way my Ma did. She lived fine, not the way you live, but just as good when it came to cannin' things and keepin' things clean."

Moe Sykes on MKR's canned huckleberries,
Cross Creek, 115–16

We have cane-grindings and syrup-boilings, festive occasions when the children may run and shriek as they please and the old folks come and renew their childhoods. There are experts among the syrup boilers, and when these give a boiling, their followers flock to them.

Cross Creek, 307–8

The juice gushed from the spout into a wooden bucket. It was green and clouded. Children dipped tin cups into its thin sweetness and ran away into corners to drink. The juice was chilled by the November air, and it seemed as if no one could get enough.

South Moon Under, 300

"The law says I cain't shoot a buck in my own potato patch! . . . The law says I cain't kill me a wild turkey scratchin' up my cowpeas. The law this, the law that! Why, . . . I'm too old a man to begin obeyin' the law!"

Cal Long, *Cross Creek*, 236

Now he realized that he was lost. As a boy he had hunted these woods, but always with other boys and men. He had gone through them unseeing, stretching his young muscles luxuriously, absorbing lazily the rich Florida sun, cooling his face at every running branch. His shooting had been careless, avid. He liked to see the brown birds tumble in midair. He liked to hunt with the pack, to gorge on the game dinners they cooked by lake shores under oak trees. When the group turned homeward, he followed, thinking of supper; of the 'shine his old man kept hidden in the smokehouse; of the girls he knew. Someone else knew north and south, and the cross patterns of the piney-woods roads. The lonely region was now as unfamiliar as though he had been a stranger.

"Gal Young Un," *Short Stories*, 151

Our first-day-of-season hunt is a glorified combination lighthearted search after deer, squirrel and quail. We set out for the big scrub about four o'clock in the morning.

Cross Creek, 315

"Huntin's a man's business, ain't it Pa, even on Christmas?"

Jody, *The Yearling*, 338

We prefer to crab-hunt on a night when the moon rises late. We work in darkness down to the mouth of the run, where the water hyacinths mass against the current, then paddle upstream with our catch in the moonlight.

Cross Creek, 230

The clearing itself was pleasant if the unweeded rows of young shafts of corn were not before him. The wild bees had found the chinaberry tree by the front gate. They burrowed into the fragile clusters of lavender bloom as greedily as though there were no other flowers in the scrub; as though they had forgotten the yellow jasmine of March; the sweet bay and the magnolias ahead of them in May. It occurred to him that he might follow the swift line of flight of the black and gold bodies, and so find a bee-tree, full of amber honey. . . . The afternoon was alive with a soft stirring. It bored into him as the bees bored into the chinaberry blossoms.

The Yearling, 1–2

Five years of planting had levelled the soil of the clearing. Sugar-cane and corn had flattened the fields. Sweet potatoes had been hilled and the hills knocked down again for the digging. Planting, growth and harvest; planting, growth and harvest; they had smoothed the sandy loam to a counterpane flung down between scrub and hammock.

South Moon Under, 31

"Good God, with a bounty
Look down on Marion County,

For the soil is so pore, and so awfully rooty, too,
I don't know what to God the pore folks gonna do."

Mo Jacklin, *South Moon Under*, 21

He heard the shouts of men above distant axes and cross-cut saws. The drum on the pull-boat chattered, the gears ground and creaked. A steam whistle blew, the engine puffed and chugged. The great cypress began to fall. Three hundred feet away he saw a trembling in the dark canopy that was the tree-tops over the swamp. There came a ripping, as woody cells, inseparable for a century, were torn violently one from another. The tree crashed, flattening everything in its path, and the roar of the fall went like a roll of thunder through swamp and hammock and scrub.

South Moon Under, 63

A man could work himself to skin and bones, so that there was no flesh left on him to make sweat in the sun, and a crop would get away from him. There was something about all living that was uncertain.

South Moon Under, 36

It was hard to think of the trapping and the farm work and the garden. He felt unsteady on his feet, as though the earth were liquid. His mind moved forward to February and March and April, but the core of his body still drifted on the river.

South Moon Under, 168–69

The planting continued all week. Cow-peas followed the corn and cotton. Sweet potatoes followed the cow-peas.

The vegetable garden back of the house was planted to onions and turnips, for the moon was dark, and root crops must be planted then.

The Yearling, 389

The planting itself was done, but he was not content. He was in a fever over the spring work, for weather conditions were favorable and the year's living depended on the immediate results.

The Yearling, 389

It was April. The whip-poor-wills had been calling for a month. The cane was well advanced, but he was only now planting his field corn. Crows made question and answer in the neighboring hammock, waiting for the seed to fall. The birds interrogated raucously the man and mule moving steadily, sideways to the high sun. The corn dropped like gold nuggets from the horse planter. The crows would drift down like shining leaves of burned paper and would dig it up again.

South Moon Under, 31

Summer

Folk who have never known a tropical summer have never luxuriated in indolence, while the world around them burst out of its sheath in a mad exuberance of growth.

Cross Creek, 268

We have little advance news of summer. One day it is spring, with the air cool and the buds still opening. The next, it is summer, and the sun is very close to the earth, and the redbirds lift their wings and open their bills to cool themselves.

Cross Creek, 269

He supposed June was a fine month everywhere. Roads all over the country would be lined with flowering thorn and hazel. Birds would be nesting clear to California. The roads would be stony in places, or made of clay, or churn into a fine powder like flour, but they would all feel good under a man's feet. They would feel good to the hoofs of a horse.

The Sojourner, 105

Dessie Smith Vinson (later Prescott) in 1933, the year she and Rawlings traveled on the St. Johns River, an adventure recounted in "Hyacinth Drift." Courtesy of the Department of Special and Area Studies Collections, George A. Smathers Libraries, University of Florida.

At this time, in late July, the crêpe myrtles were in full bloom. Several had been trained into single-stemmed, small trees, the tops a riotous mass of pink, lavender, or red, like flowered parasols. In one corner the oldest myrtle had been permitted to grow in its own fashion, a dense many-based shrub twenty feet in height. It was thick with gray Spanish moss. The flowers it bore were white and it stood alone in a hoary antiquity.

Golden Apples, 146

The shade of the oak was cool. A light breeze moved through its leaves. Jody's shaggy hair was wet. He pushed it out of his eyes and wiped his face on his blue sleeve, then settled himself to quiet. Silence took over the scrub. Far away a hawk cried shrilly and was gone. No bird stirred in any branches. No creature moved or fed. No bees droned, or any insect. It was high noon.

The Yearling, 103–4

I shall always associate my conception of hell with hot Sunday summer mornings at the Creek. And why Sunday morning? Because that is when the drinking portion of the Negro help fails to arrive.

Cross Creek, 111

"Never grieve for me. Only think sometime, when summer wind blow, 'Ah, the Old One, she speaks to me!'"

The Old One, *The Sojourner*, 240

The days were hot and humid. Penny sweat in his bed. Buck came dripping from the fields. He discarded his shirt and worked naked to the waist. His chest was thick with black hair. The perspiration glistened on it like rain drops on black dried moss. When she was sure he would not call for it, Ma Baxter washed and boiled the shirt and hung it in the scalding sunshine.

The Yearling, 178–79

The scrub lay parching under an August sun. The wiregrass was brown and dry. The scrub pines quivered in the heat, their taproots pushing desperately lower for a water that was not there. The desiccated needles gave forth an aromatic scent as acrid as though they were being broiled. The sand underfoot was slippery, like fine glass.

South Moon Under, 121

The mosquitoes descended on me. One would think that exposed neck, arms and face, would suffice the hungriest of insects. But a mosquito is Freudian, taking delight only in the hidden places. They wavered with their indecisive flight up under my skirts and stabbed me in the poison ivy, in the nutritional rash, around the sandspurs, and settled with hums of joy in all unoccupied small places. It was too much.

Cross Creek, 12

He lay down on his pallet and drew the fawn down beside him. He often lay so with it in the shed, or under the live oaks in the heat of the day.

The Yearling, 192

August was merciless in its heat, but it was, mercifully, leisurely. There was little work to be done and no great hurry about the doing of that little.

The Yearling, 214

The grove itself seems safe and open. . . . There are times when the evening sun infiltrates so eerily the dense summer cover crop under the orange trees that the green growth seems, not vegetation, but sea, emerald green, with the light seeming to come from high distant earthly places down through the luminous waters.

Cross Creek, 35

The first week in September was as parched and dry as old bones. Only the weeds grew. There was a tension in the heat. The dogs were snappish. The snakes were crawling, dog days being past, and their shedding and their blindness ended.

The Yearling, 220

Flora

The Glisson house, home of Rawlings's next-door neighbors at Cross Creek.
Courtesy of the Department of Special and Area Studies Collections,
George A. Smathers Libraries, University of Florida.

There is no such thing in the world as an ugly tree, but the *magnolia grandiflora* has a unique perfection. No matter how crowded it may be, no matter how thickly holly and live oak and sweet gum may grow up around it, it develops with complete symmetry, so that one wonders whether character in all things, human as well as vegetable, may not be implicit.

Cross Creek, 28–29

He had bought . . . high good land in the center of a pine island. The island was called by such a name, in an arid forest, because it was literally an island of long-leaf pines, lifted high, a landmark, in the rolling sea of scrub. There were other such islands scattered to the north and west, where some accident of soil or moisture produced patches of luxuriant growth; even of hammock, the richest growth of all. Live oaks were here and there; the red bay and the magnolia; wild cherry and sweet gum; hickory and holly.

The Yearling, 18–19

The undergrowth was thick, laced with cat-briers. Then hammock, too, ended, and to the south and west lay a broad open expanse that looked at first sight to be a meadow. This was the saw-grass. It grew knee-deep in water, its harsh saw-edged blades rising so thickly that it seemed a compact vegetation.

The Yearling, 33

We at the Creek need and have found only very simple things. We must need flowering and fruiting trees, for all of us have citrus groves of one size or another. We must need a certain blandness of season, with a longer and more beneficent heat than many require, for there is never too much sun for us, and through the long summers we do not complain. We need the song of birds, and there is none finer than the redbird. We need the sound of rain coming across the *hamaca*, and the sound of wind in trees—and there is no more sensitive Aeolian harp than the palm.

Cross Creek, 3

The Spanish moss sways a little as always. The heavy forest thins into occasional great trees, live oaks and palms and pines. In the spring, the yellow jessamine is heavy on the air, in summer the red trumpet vine shouts from the gray trucks, and in autumn and winter the holly berries are small bright lamps in the half-light.

Cross Creek, 37

A magnolia sixty feet tall shaded the tenant house. It was covered from top to bottom with tall white candles that burst wide into dazzling glories, opening from the top down, like a Christmas tree being slowly lighted. The blossoming was leisurely. The great white blooms were above her head for weeks. Then the white petals began to drop down and turn russet on the ground.

"Jacob's Ladder," *Short Stories*, 69

The blooms, for all their size and thickness, are as delicate as orchids in that they reject the touch of human hands. They must be cut or broken carefully and placed in a jar of water without brushing the edges, or the creamy petals will turn in an hour to brown velvet. Properly handled, they open in the house as on the tree, the cupped buds bursting open suddenly, the full-blown flowers shedding the red-tipped stamens in a shower, so that in a quiet room you hear them sifting onto the table top. The red seed cones are as fine as candles. They mature slowly from the top of the tree down, as a Christmas tree is lighted.

Cross Creek, 29–30

I invariably put off all the orange picking as long as possible. I have watched the fruit so long, from the first blossoms in February, through the summer growth of the hard green balls, through the sudden swelling on the fall rains, and, with cool nights, the bright color showing. The oranges hang like lighted lanterns through the winter.

Cross Creek, 324

The down grade tempted him to a lope. He reached the thick-bedded sand of Silver Glen road. The tar-flower was in bloom, and fetter-bush and sparkleberry. . . . He reached the magnolia tree where he had carved the wild-cat's face. The growth was a sign that there was water nearby. It seemed a strange thing to him, when earth was earth and rain was rain, that scrawny pines should grow in the scrub, while by every branch and lake and river there grew magnolias.

The Yearling, 3

The orange groves were fabulous. They rolled away to the horizon, losing themselves at last in tawny marshes. A rim of blue was the lake beyond them. The orange trees were dark and rounded. They were hung, miraculously, with round and golden globes. The rows of trees marched in dark aisles, and to the west and east were endless.

Golden Apples, 236

The oranges and tangerines, the spicier grapefruit, the wild-rose-like bloom of the thorny trifoliate, drenched the world with their sweetness. The scent was more powerful at night. As soon as the sun withdrew its dryness, the bloom sent its odor into every nook and cranny of the air. It was inescapable. Still weak and dizzy, for weeks she dropped off to sleep at night, drowning in perfumed waters.

"Jacob's Ladder," *Short Stories*, 69

The combs of apple blossom honey would be recognizable, pale as April sunlight. The bean blossom honey would be nearly the color of Amelia's amber beads. Clover honey, later, would be the color of the brook water beneath the willows, the goldenrod again would darken, and last would come the buckwheat honey, red black, strong and pungent, and his favorite.

The Sojourner, 106

When, in late April or early May, the pale buds unfold into great white waxy blossoms, sometimes eight or ten inches across, and the perfume is a delirious thing on the spring air, I would not trade one tree for a conservatory filled with orchids.

Cross Creek, 29

The first orange blossoms have opened. For a month or six weeks we shall be giddy by day with them and at night drown in a sea of perfume.

Cross Creek, 246

She looked to him like a ruffled blue gentian and her breath was sweet with wintergreen leaves she had gathered on her way. The hemlock needles were a soft and fragrant bed. The April breeze had lifted the hemlock boughs in a rocking motion, the earth had spun under them in one direction and the blue April sky had reeled over them in another. They had been almost too dizzy to stand.

The Sojourner, 120

Rawlings and her maid Martha Mickens, early 1930s. Courtesy of the
Department of Special and Area Studies Collections, George A. Smathers
Libraries, University of Florida.

7
· · · · · ·

Plenty and Want

For all its shabbiness, this was a land of plenty.
Golden Apples, 179

Jody heard nothing; saw nothing but his plate. He had
never been so hungry in his life, and after a lean winter
and slow spring, with food not much more plentiful
for the Baxters than for their stock, his mother had
cooked a supper good enough for the preacher. There
were poke-greens with bits of white bacon buried in
them; sand-buggers made of potato and onion and the
cooter he had found crawling yesterday; sour orange
biscuits and at his mother's elbow the sweet potato
pone. He was torn between his desire for more biscuits
and another sand-bugger and the knowledge, born of
painful experience, that if he ate them, he would suddenly have no room for pone. The choice was plain.
The Yearling, 12

The summer apples were sweetening under their thin
rosy skins. Wild strawberries had been eaten with thick
golden cream, made into extravagant tarts and short-

cakes, preserved in the sun, and were now done with. Huckleberries and blueberries made puddings and pies. The hedges were thick with blackberries and the birds quarreled with the Lindens over their gathering. Wild raspberries were ripening in thick and almost inaccessible tangles.

The Sojourner, 128

There was fried chicken, which Nellie did not believe in saving only for Sundays. There were sweet corn and small new potatoes, wax beans swimming in butter and cream, hot biscuits and sliced tomatoes, cucumbers in vinegar with rings of onion, and the usual assortment of relishes and jelly. The noon of the day had turned fresh and cool. The white curtains blew from the open windows. Full sun broke through and streamed across the damasked table.

The Sojourner, 155

The sand was like powder. The clay ridges were burned brick. The flat-woods were brown. The occasional hammocks were dried up except in the lowest swamps and along the edges of lakes and streams. The creeks were withered down to the brown beds, cracking wide with thirst. The frogs, who had sung all spring in the good damp, were silent under the ooze where they had burrowed. Across the roads the moccasins and king snakes moved all day in search of water. Now the winds had stopped, and there was no breath of coolness anywhere. September was so still, so hot, that the very elements could not endure it.

"Jacob's Ladder," *Short Stories*, 102

The smoke-house was dark and cool, odorous with the smell of hams and bacons, dusty with the ash of hickory. The rafters, studded with square-headed nails for the hanging of meats, were now almost bare. Three shoulders of ham hung, lean and withered, and two bacon sides. A haunch of jerked venison swung beside the smoked alligator meat. . . . Jody hacked away a piece of alligator. The meat was dry but tender. He touched his tongue to it. Its saltiness was not unpleasing.

The Yearling, 30

"You're a plague-taken ninny, that's what you be. Leave them wild things kill our stock cold-blooded, and us starve to death. But no, you're too tender to give 'em a belly-ache."

"Pizen jest someway ain't natural. Tain't fair fightin'."

Ma to Penny and Penny to Jody, *The Yearling*, 287

It was a time of pride in a season of abundance, and apple dumplings and blackberry puddings and wild raspberry shortcakes jostled the pies and the layer cakes for attention. The block of lake ice from the sawdust of the ice-house was chipped into more iced tea, more coffee was poured, the greediest man of all could hold no more, and the table was bare. The cry went up, "Clean the table and kiss the cook!"

The Sojourner, 134

The corn matured, the shocks stood like teepees in the field, the pumpkins were enormous around them, the Hubbard squash big and noduled and firm. Squash, pumpkins, turnips, beets and carrots went to the root-cellar. Cabbage was shredded and put down in five-gallon crocks to make sauerkraut, made into a relish, stuffed inside green peppers put down in herb-seasoned cider vinegar. Popcorn was hung in bunches festooned on strings on the upper floor of the carriage house. Hogs were butchered, lard and sausage made, hams and bacons hung in the brick smoke-house over slow hickory coals. Nuts were gathered, hickory, hazel, black walnut, beech and butternut. They lay in piles under the popcorn to make a delight of winter evenings before the fire.

The Sojourner, 138

"Everybody brings a pound of something. Sugar, or butter, or candy, or a cake. A cake's fine. Such as that."

Ella May defines a "pound party," *Cross Creek*, 41

Ma Forrester banged a pot-lid and lifted a pan of corn-bread as big, Jody thought, as a syrup kettle. The good smells from the hearth were overwhelming. . . . She ladled food into pans big enough to wash in. The long trenchered table was covered with steam. There were dried cow-peas boiled with white bacon, a haunch of roast venison, a platter of fried squirrel, swamp cabbage, big hominy, biscuits, cornbread, syrup and coffee. A raisin pudding waited at the side of the hearth.

The Yearling, 56

"I don't go to the doin's often, and when I do go, I aim not to go scarce."

Ma, *The Yearling*, 330

The Baxters went into the scrub for flesh of deer and hide of wild-cat. And the predatory animals and the hungry varmints came into the clearing when they could. The clearing was ringed around with hunger. It was a fortress in the scrub. Baxter's Island was an island of plenty in a hungry sea.

The Yearling, 142

Fire

There had been no forest fire. The flames that licked at times through the adjacent pine woods and across Sawgrass Prairie drooped like thirsty and exhausted tongues at the edge of the cool dampness. No timber had been cut. No axe had rung against the silence. Live oak and magnolia, sweet gum and hickory, mulberry and ironwood, red bay and holly, all reached their ultimate height and vastness. Here and there a patriarch rotted in dignity and quiet and its saplings sprouted about its roots in the rich dust of its decay.

Golden Apples, 17

The first heavy frost came at the end of November. The leaves of the big hickory at the north end of the clearing turned as yellow as butter. The sweet gums were yellow and red and the black-jack thicket across the road from the house flamed with a red as bright as a camp-fire.

The Yearling, 279

"You don't figger on fire in November."

Cleve, *South Moon Under*, 237

But the summer had been dry, frost had come early, and the scrub was like tinder. The floor was carpeted with parched brown pine needles. Dead palmetto fronds were like oil-soaked paper. Old lighter'd knots and fallen pine limbs made a network of inflammability.

South Moon Under, 237

In the morning the great fire would be built under the syrup kettle and the juice would be boiled down in forty-gallon lots. The grinding and boiling would go on for two or three weeks. Today and tonight folk drank and laughed and children ran and romped.

South Moon Under, 301

A bonfire burned between the mill and the house for light and warmth. Boys foraged about the yard and down the road and threw on dry palmetto fronds and dog-fennel to make it blaze. Half a dozen couples detached themselves from the light, like shadows shifting, and ran into the house to join the set that was forming for the square-dance. Two or three older pairs entered the circle and stood with linked hands to wait for the calling.

South Moon Under, 303

All wood was wet, but, prowling about, he found a fallen pine whose core was rich with resin. . . . It would make a burning base to dry out the other wood. They chopped it in half and laid the two long pieces side by side. Jody struggled with flint and steel from the tinder horn until Penny took it away from him and kindled a fire between the logs with fatwood splinters. He piled on small brush that caught fire quickly. Larger limbs and logs were added. They smoked and smoldered but ended by bursting into flame.

The Yearling, 249

The camp site was desolate. The charred logs, the gray ashes, were forlorn. The magic had died out with the flames of the camp-fire. The morning had been cool but the climbing sun began to heat the day. The earth steamed.

The Yearling, 259

The circle of distant lake was a red fire. The sun dipped suddenly into the west. The sky flamed and was violent. Every orange tree had for a moment its bright identity. There was an instant when the earth faltered between night and day. The ibis were white feathers at the marsh edge. A bat flew low under the magnolia in search of insects. Then all the world was shadow.

Golden Apples, 247

I have seen no more beautiful thing in my life than my orange grove by night, lighted by the fatwood fires. It is doubly beautiful for the danger and the struggle, like a beloved friend for whose life one battles, drinking in the well known features that may be taken away forever.

Cross Creek, 335

The pine burns with a bright orange flame and the effect is of countless bivouac fires across a low-wooded plain. The sky is sapphire blue, spangled with stars. The smoke lifts from the fires gray-white, melting into gray-blue, drifting like the veils of a dancer under the open skies. Each orange tree is outlined with light. The green leaves shine like jade. The round golden oranges are each lit with a secret inner candle.

Cross Creek, 336

Smoke from the camp-fire eddied up and joined the stars. He watched it drift through the pine tops. His eyelids fluttered. He did not want to go to sleep. He wanted to listen. The hunting talk of men was the finest talk in the world. Chills went along his spine to hear it. The smoke against the stars was a veil drawn back and forth across his eyes. He closed them. For a moment the talk of the men was a deep droning against the snapping of the wet wood. Then it faded into the sound of the breeze in the pines, and was no longer sound, but the voiceless murmur of a dream.

The Yearling, 255

The smoke darkened and grew thicker. A black cloud billowed towards the sky. The wind was from the west. It took the smoke in its sweep and spread it thinly over the scrub.

South Moon Under, 311

Half an hour later she heard the sound of axes on wood and metal. The noise diminished and the west wind brought to her nose the smell of things burning that had not burned before. She knew the odours of burning pine, sweet and aromatic; of hammock, green and pre-mature; of broom sage, that burned like paper. There was in the air an acridity that was unfamiliar. Then even her dim sight discerned the smoke, a broad col-umn that reared from below the hammock ledge. It was rank and dark, as though the swamp itself were burning. The Prohis were at Lant's still.

South Moon Under, 311–12

Only a pillar of fire by night would have seemed suf-ficient comfort and guidance, and this was never pro-vided except by the dubious assistance of lightning.

On the path to the outhouse, *Cross Creek*, 59

They went together to the swamp and looked at the ruins. The platform over the creek had made a fine bon-fire for the barrels and the cooker. Nothing was left but twisted metal and blackened bricks. The trees in the swamp had burned for forty feet around, and the flames had licked far up into the hammock. Sweet gum and magnolia and hickory and palm stood sick and charred.

South Moon Under, 313–14

Only a hunting dog or a cat can share man's love of the open fire, and if I had a whole kennel full of dogs, on winter nights I should let them all come in to enjoy mine with me.

Cross Creek, 340–41

A fresh log of fatwood thrown on the slow-burning bed of oak coals catches and blazes and roars up the big

chimney. The flames light the old white-walled room so that there is no need even of candles, though one or two over the bookshelves are always pleasant, for candlelight on books is one of the lovely things of this world.

Cross Creek, 340

9
· · · · · ·

Sound and Silence

Rawlings on the dunes at her Crescent Beach cottage, early 1940s. Photograph
by Jacob Lofman. Courtesy of the Department of Special and Area Studies
Collections, George A. Smathers Libraries, University of Florida.

The sound, once heard, can never be forgotten and is always recognizable for what it is. . . . The roar becomes a booming and the path of the wind is visible far ahead. . . . There is not the coziness of being shut in away from ordinary storms. Too gigantic a force is at large for any sense of safety.

Cross Creek, 306

The music was out of tune and thunderous. It sounded like all the wild-cats in the scrub rounded up together, but it had a rhythm and a gusto that satisfied the ear and soul. The wild chords went through Jody as though he too were a fiddle and Lem Forrester drew long fingers across him.

The Yearling, 67

The wrens and jorees were noisiest, until woodpeckers and flickers began to drum. There were few songbirds. The scrub was too vast, too lonely, too desolate, for song. Only the solitary note of the thrush sounded, infinitely sweet and sad and forgotten.

South Moon Under, 124

"The fiddle cain't play without the bow."

Penny, *The Yearling*, 226

Redbirds were everywhere, dropping from limb to limb like blossoms of the trumpet vine blowing with the wind. Their song filled the wild grove, sweeter, Luke thought, than honey on the tongue.

Golden Apples, 62

He was a drunken little old Irishman from the bogs of Aran, a hired farm hand by necessity, a fiddler by the grace of God and to the glory of man.

The Sojourner, 18

The quail were nesting. The fluted covey call had been silent for some time. The coveys were dividing into pairs. The cocks were sounding the mating call, clear and sweet and insistent.

The Yearling, 139

The peace of the vast aloof scrub had drawn him with the beneficence of its silence. Something in him was raw and tender. The touch of men was hurtful upon it, but the touch of the pines was healing. . . . The wild animals seemed less predatory to him than people he had known. The forays of bear and wolf and wild-cat and panther on the stock were understandable, which was more than he could say of human cruelties.

The Yearling, 18

In the beginning there was a chatter of talk, the children scrambling, and then the gypsy song took over, and spoke to each man, each woman. The tremulous violin made the young uneasy. Was love to prove so sad as this? The flute cried to the elders. One wrinkled hand groped to find another. Had love been after all so sweet? So sad, so sweet, the ancient song assured them. The last note faded away, to be a ghost again.

The Sojourner, 28

The rhythm of the dance was joy, its community was release. The ancient ones swore they had never been less tired, the lovers wandered away to corners, the children slid and swooped and jostled one another. The music was insistent, the dance almost too intense, and it ended sharply.

The Sojourner, 27

Her tone was jovial. Jody liked her. Women ran in breeds, like dogs, he thought. She was of Grandma Hutto's breed, that made men easy. And two women could say the same words and the meaning would not be the same, as the bark of two dogs, one menacing and the other friendly.

Jody on Nellie Ginright, *The Yearling,* 345

At night there is singing in the Mickens house, for the slow time is the time for song, and Little Will's guitar is strummed softly, the sound as soft as the summer air.

Cross Creek, 271

The frog Philharmonic of the Florida lakes and marshes is unendurable in its sweetness. I have lain through a long moonlit night, with the scent of orange blossoms palpable as spilled perfume on the air, and listened to the murmur of minor chords until . . . I thought my heart would break with the beauty of it.

Cross Creek, 144–45

The roar of a bull 'gator was like thunder in the heart of solitude. The gray and green and red of the distant hammock merged to form the semblance of tall cliffs, like prehistoric walls. The palms topped them like shaggy heads, far away. The blue sky was illimitable. Except for the rain-like rush of the coots and the dip of the paddle, the lake was a blue pool of silence.

"Jacob's Ladder," *Short Stories*, 60

An hour before sunrise the girl Piety was awakened by the throaty cries of hoot-owls. The great night-birds had seldom sounded in the piney-woods. The bare pines were not to their liking. They preyed on small creatures that fed in the richness of marsh and hammock. Their cry was stirring, like a thick sob. It rose in a rhythmic crescendo, subsiding in agony in a minor key.

South Moon Under, 11

A layer of thin sunlight reached across the clearing. It was shot with lines of mist. A redbird began to sing. Its song split the morning air with bright bars of sound. There were two worlds: the world when the redbird sang: the world when the bird was silent. The palm heads showed, swathed in vapor. A light wind stirred and they shook themselves free of it. Mist hung from them an instant, as the Spanish moss hung from the live oaks. Then the fog was gone. The redbird sang, dissolved in a liquid ecstasy. The sun flooded the clearing.

Golden Apples, 262

There is a sibilant sound in the pecan trees, the grayness thickens, and rain marches visibly across palms and orange trees and comes in at the gate. Sometimes it is a gentle shower, sometimes a rushing flood. After it has passed, the air is as fresh and clean as April and the night will be cool for sleeping.

Cross Creek, 274–75

The hammock was clamorous with the cries of birds. Trumpet vines were breaking into waves of scarlet bloom. The business of growth went forward, with color and song. The explosion of birth, the violence of life, the simmering droop of dying like a rocket falling, it was all and only bright flowers on the one great vine; moments of song, harmonious or dissonant, it made no difference, in the major symphony.

Golden Apples, 330

Wisdom

There is a strange communion between a boy and a dog. Perhaps they possess the same singleness of spirit, the same kind of wisdom. It is difficult to explain, but it exists.

    "A Mother in Mannville," *Short Stories*, 246

"A boy ain't a boy too long."

        Penny, *The Yearling*, 16

"Four times the deer feeds. Stirs or feeds. Moon-rise and moon-down, and south-moon-over and south-moon-under."

    Old Man Paine, *South Moon Under*, 100

"A mornin' rain is like an old woman's dance—soon over."

    Martha Mickens, *Cross Creek*, 302

"No use to butcher on a wanin' moon. The meat jest shrivels in the fryin' pan. Quare, the way the moon do things, ain't it?"

      Kezzy, *South Moon Under*, 189

"You can't trust nothin' is free."

    Mrs. Townsend, *Cross Creek*, 46

"Three things bring a man home again—his bed, his woman, and his dinner."

Doc, *The Yearling*, 166

"You cain't git all your 'coons up one tree."

Penny, *The Yearling*, 70

"But a gal cain't belong to two fellers at oncet."
"You jest don't know gals."

Jody and Buck, *The Yearling*, 168

"You belong to figger. A wild creetur's quicker'n and a heap stronger. What's a man got that a bear ain't got? A mite more sense. He cain't out-run a bear, but he's a sorry hunter if he cain't out-study him."

Penny, *The Yearling*, 32

It's a wonderful thing just to set down and figure out how many different ways there are to be crazy.

Quincey Dover, "Benny and the Bird Dogs,"
Short Stories, 208

"Nothin' ain't safe ner sartin exscusin' a iron pot o' gold or siller, put deep in a place where nobody else cain't find hit."

Drenna, "A Crop of Beans," *Short Stories*, 147

"You have to frail all the young uns to git the right un. . . . Start with a big un and end with the least un."

A mother of ten, *South Moon Under*, 301

"That ain't no beggar. That's a person."

Martha Mickens, *Cross Creek*, 25

"Well, I know better than to question a good dog's sense."

Penny, *The Yearling*, 266

"Take it easy, men, slower you work on this, better we'll do."

Penny, *The Yearling*, 298

"Chile, antses is fine fo' the stummick-ache."

Martha Mickens, *Cross Creek*, 153

"A young 'coon for runnin'—but a ol' 'coon for cunnin'."

Zeke, *South Moon Under*, 99

"Clothes washes easier, anyways, on a cloudy day. My Ma allus said, 'Soft weather, soft clothes.'"

Ma, *The Yearling*, 222

"Some folks say a dog can't smell good with gravy on his nose, . . . but a dog ain't goin' to leave no gravy on his nose."

Fred Tompkins, *Cross Creek*, 318–19

"I'd rather sleep with a moccasin over each shoulder than get caught in a hyacinth block."

Dessie, *Cross Creek*, 356

Autumn

Somehow "autumn" does not seem properly used of Florida. There is a connotation in the word of flaming color, of sharp change, of hoar frost heavy on cornfields, of all of northern harvest. The sub-tropical fall is so impalpable, so much a protraction of summer, pendulous before the time of winter fruiting, that we might almost say that we have no such season.

Cross Creek, 298

The fall fruits were not yet ripe, papaw and gallberry and persimmon. The mast of the pines, the acorns of the oaks, the berries of the palmetto, would not be ready until the first frost. The deer were feeding on the tender growth, bud of sweet bay and of myrtle, sprigs of wire-grass, tips of arrow-root in the ponds and prairies, and succulent lily stems and pads. The type of food kept them in the low, wet places.

The Yearling, 221

The month was October. The summer had seemed long. There had been as yet no sharp break in the heat. Equinoctial storms, due in mid-September, had not blown in

Rawlings at the Cross Creek grove gate, circa 1939. Photograph by Mrs. Fred E. (Eva) Noble. Courtesy of the Department of Special and Area Studies Collections, George A. Smathers Libraries, University of Florida.

from the Caribbean. The high temperatures had moderated, yet the air, that should have been crisp and fresh, was lifeless. The broom-sage was brown, the fennel desiccated, the lush coffee-weed withering. The purple flowers of the deer-tongue were going into seed.

Golden Apples, 164–65

The grapevines were golden and the sumac was like oak embers. The October blooming of dog-fennel and sea-myrtle had turned to a feathery fluff. The days came in, cool and crisp, warmed to a pleasant slowness and chilled again.

The Yearling, 279

When the dog fennel blooms, we count that it will be forty days until frost. When the curlews wheel, high in the sky, we are despondent, for they are called the dry-weather birds, and the circling flocks indicate that the fall rains are a long time away.

Cross Creek, 299

Spring and fall seldom produce fog, for the variance of temperature then is slight. The fog is a combination of beauty and nightmare.

Cross Creek, 289

October was over and done, the more anxious birds were winging south, ducks and geese stopped for rest and feeding in the marshes beyond the willow-bordered stream. The poplar trees were last to loose their leaves. They quivered in anguish above the yellow piles that blew here and there in the harsh November wind.

The Sojourner, 132–33

The weather had been unseasonable since October, when the autumn storms failed to appear. The dry heat of summer had continued on past Christmas. The mosquitoes thrived through January and February, with no rain, no cold, to kill them. It was impossible to raise anything in the garden.

South Moon Under, 111

By November, the Baxters and the Forresters knew the extent of the plague and what to expect, both of the game and the predatory animals, during the winter.

The Yearling, 271

Rations

"Hit'll do you no harm to learn to be keerful. You got to learn takin' keer o' rations comes first of all—first after gittin' 'em."

Penny, *The Yearling*, 278

There are elevated Floridians who turn up their noses at hush-puppies, but any huntsman would not exchange a plate of them for crêpes suzettes.

Cross Creek, 209

Hush-puppies have a background, which is more than many fancy breads can claim. Back of them is the hunt, the fishing trip, the camaraderie, the grease in the Dutch oven aromatic to hungry sportsmen. . . . The name? It came, old-timers say, from hunting trips of long ago, when the hunters sat or stood around the camp fire and the Negro cooks and helpers sweat over their cooking and the hunters ate lustily. And although the hunting dogs tethered to nearby trees had been fed their evening meal, they smelled the good smells of man's victuals, and tugged at their leashes, and whined

Martha Mickens and Idella Parker, Rawlings's maids, preparing a meal in the kitchen at Cross Creek. Courtesy of the Department of Special and Area Studies Collections, George A. Smathers Libraries, University of Florida.

for a tid-bit extra. Then cook or helper or huntsman would toss the left-over little corn patties to the dogs, calling, "Hush, puppies!" And the dogs bolted the toothsome morsels and hushed, in their great content.

Cross Creek, 209–10

"Why the meat's so tender, . . . you could kiss it off the bones."

Penny on Ma's squirrel pilau, *The Yearling*, 392

Rattlesnake is of course eaten as a delicate hors d'œuvre, but of all the queer things I have served or eaten, this alone is not among them. It is sheer prejudice, no doubt, but I know too well the heavy, rolling black and yellow bodies to relish a morsel from their midriffs.

Cross Creek, 207

"Be cooter eggs fitten fer folks to eat?" she inquired distastefully.
"I mean!"

Florry and Mart, "Jacob's Ladder," *Short Stories*, 54

"Jest you wait 'twel you sees what happens in the pan."
"[D]ogged iffen I wants to eat anything you has to stand on the lid to keep it poppin' out o' the pan."

Mart and Florry on frog legs,
"Jacob's Ladder," *Short Stories*, 54

"The longer you chaw . . . the bigger it gets."

Fred Tompkins on frog legs, *Cross Creek*, 148

Better men than I have written lyrically about the mango. They have also written, to my notion, abusively, for they insist that the only way to eat a mango is in a bathing suit by the side of the ocean or in the bathtub. This maligns the mango.

Cross Creek, 218

"I don't belong to be skeert. . . . You done tole me your very self, hit don't make no difference where we goes nor what we does, not where we squats to eat our rations."

"Iffen we got any—."

Florry and Mart, "Jacob's Ladder," *Short Stories*, 100

"Well, I'd a heap ruther you was good about rations and mean about other things."

Jody to Ma, *The Yearling*, 294

An unhappy combination is collard greens and hog chitlings. Rural Florida is divided into chitling and anti-chitling camps and feelings sometimes runs high. Man stands against wife and mother against child.

Cross Creek, 214

I speak with some trepidation of my blackbird pie, for it might have brought down on me Federal dishonor, or roughly speaking, jail.

Cross Creek, 232

I slipped No. 10 shells into my shotgun, and two shots brought down a dozen birds. I made the dozen very secretly into a pie. It was utterly delicious.

Cross Creek, 232

We are all in complete agreement on squirrel meat. Fried, smother-fried with a rich gravy, or made into a pilau, we esteem it highly. There are, however, strong differences of opinion on the edibility of the head.

Cross Creek, 240

I shall not forget the early Christmas afternoon, with six men gathered for dinner, the turkey savory in the oven, the pies cooling, the vegetables ready, the necessity if not the desire for the bath borne in on me, and the temperature at thirty-eight and dropping. I emerged shivering and snarled at the indifferent heavens, "The first time I get my hands on cash money, so help me, I shall have a bathroom."

Cross Creek, 57

"I want a gallon o' your best 'shine, dogged if I don't. Time you drink some good 'shine, you don't notice if you've got nothin' else."

Kezzy's Christmas wish, *South Moon Under*, 265

We stopped by a pond and went swimming. The region was flat, the horizon limitless, and as I came out of the cool blue water I expected to find myself surrounded by a ring of rattlers. There were only Ross and Will, opening the lunch basket. I could not eat. Ross never touches liquor and it seemed to me that I would give my hope of salvation for a dram of whiskey.

MKR's winter snake hunt with Ross Allen
and Will Mickens, *Cross Creek*, 170–71

"Rations tastes a heap better in the woods. I'd rather eat cold bread in the woods than hot puddin' in the house."

Mill-wheel Forrester, *The Yearling*, 251

"I ain't goin' to let my imagination quarrel with what goes in my belly."

Penny, *The Yearling*, 252

The game seemed for him to be two different animals. On the chase, it was the quarry. He wanted only to see it fall. When it lay dead and bleeding, he was sickened and sorry. His heart ached over the mangled death. Then when it was cut into portions, and dried and salted and smoked; or boiled or baked or fried in the savory kitchen or roasted over the camp-fire, it was only meat, like bacon, and his mouth watered at its goodness. He wondered by what alchemy it was changed, so that what sickened him one hour, maddened him with hunger, the next. It seemed as though there were either two different animals or two different boys.

The Yearling, 72

"A meal like that . . . a feller don't know what's cold-out rations and what's fancy fixin's. When I seed her face, I knowed I'd ought to of run the risk and et everything."

Moe Sykes on MKR's Christmas
dinner, *Cross Creek*, 111

13

·····

Creeturs

Rawlings feeding her ducks at Cross Creek, 1950. Photograph by Alan M. Anderson. Courtesy of the Department of Special and Area Studies Collections, George A. Smathers Libraries, University of Florida.

"'Tain't stealin', in a creetur. A creetur's got his livin' to make and he makes it the best way he kin. Same as us. Hit's panther nature and wolf nature and bear nature to kill their meat. County lines is nothin' to them, nor a man's fences. How's a creetur to know I'm dependin' on my hogs for my own rations? All he knows is, he's hongry. . . . A creetur's only doin' the same as me when I go huntin' us meat. . . . Huntin' him where he lives and beds and raises his young uns. Hit's a hard law, but it's the law. 'Kill or go hungry.'"

Penny, The Yearling, 43

They were all too tightly bound together, men and women, creatures wild and tame, flowers, fruit and leaves, to ask that any one be spared.

The Sojourner, 143

"And the Lord God said unto the serpent, Because thou hast done this, thou art cursed above all cattle, and above every beast of the field; upon thy belly thou shalt go, and dust shalt thou eat all the days of thy life: And I will put enmity between thee and the woman."

Cross Creek, 166; Genesis 3:14–15

Of "all them wild things out in the woods," the panther remains the only one in Florida still gilded with the bright legend of fear. To hear a panther scream is to add a new horror to the catalogue of evil.

Cross Creek, 157

Dinghy the Scotty hated the Florida backwoods from the first sandspur under his tail. He hated the sun, he hated the people, black and white, he hated the roominess of the farmhouse and the long quiet of the nights. From the beginning, he sat on his fat Scotch behind and glowered.

Cross Creek, 31–32

Near Busby marsh, turtle doves in a flock hurled themselves toward the night's watering place. Their underbodies were rosy, facing the west. Then they passed into the sunset and were at once black, as though charred to a crisp by its heatless fire. The doves wheeled and could be seen plunging to the marsh edge.

"The Pardon," *Short Stories*, 218

It is impossible to be among the woods animals on their own ground without a feeling of expanding one's own world, as when any foreign country is visited.

Cross Creek, 37–38

It was most pleasant at this moment of its fresh cutting, piled thick and yellow in the big shadowy loft. Soon the mice would breed there and squeak and scurry, the barn cats would climb the ladder to hunt them, the hens would leave their own house with its trim rows of troughs to steal their nests in the fragrant softness, having at last to be helped down ignominiously with their broods of downy biddies, to more conventional quarters.

The Sojourner, 63

Now we pass as though we were strangers. I am ashamed to face him, having used him in my loneliness, and then betrayed him. He shows no signs of recognition. His tail curves over his back. He trots with a high head, looking straight ahead. He is a work dog, and he must be about his business.

Cross Creek, 297

He lay with his head against its side. Its ribs lifted and fell with its breathing. It rested its chin on his hand. It had a few short hairs that prickled him. He had been cudgeling his wits for an excuse to bring the fawn inside at night to sleep with him, and now he had one that could not be disputed. He would smuggle it in and out as long as possible, in the name of peace. On the inevitable day when he should be discovered, what better reason was there than the menace—the constant danger, he would point out—of bears?

The Yearling, 192

"A bear that knows he's follered moves a sight faster'n one that figgers the world's his own, to prowl and feed in. . . . He's big. He ain't full weight right now, account of his stomach bein' shrunk up from layin' up, and empty. But look at that track. Hit's sizable enough to prove him. And look at the way it's deeper at the back. A deer track'll prove the same. A deer or bear that's fat and heavy'll sink in that-a-way. A leetle ol' light doe or yearlin' 'll walk tippy-toed, and you'll not see more than the front of their hooves. Oh, he's big."

Penny, *The Yearling*, 31

"A bear'll kill ary creetur cain't out-run him."

Penny, *The Yearling*, 222

There was a commotion ahead. . . . Twin bear cubs were high in a slim pine sapling, using it for a swing. The sapling was tall and limber and the yearling cubs were rocking it back and forth. Jody had swung in the same fashion. For an instant the cubs were not bears, but boys like himself. He would have liked to climb the sapling and rock with them. It bent half-way to the ground as they swung their weight, swayed upright again, then low on the other side. The cubs made now and then an amiable talking.

The Yearling, 101

The remaining bears were scrambling across the swamp like paddle boats, churning the water behind them. . . . Jody was amazed at the speed of the bulky bodies. . . . The unharmed bears were vanishing before their eyes. No game was quicker or cleverer.

The Yearling, 261

"'Gators is harmless things."

Penny, *The Yearling*, 256

"Alligators has lots o' use for teeth, . . . and the Lord takes keer o' the sons o' bitches."

Lantry, *South Moon Under*, 243

There was something fey about most of the family. Rodney [Slater], the cripple, foretold the weather with a strange accuracy. He had always some small pet, a squirrel or chameleon or perhaps a chicken hurt and crippled like himself. I think that "Fodder-wing" in *The Yearling* must have been Rodney.

Cross Creek, 73

Over all the dark hours hung the fear of snakes. I had arrived in Florida with the usual ignorant terror. If time proved that the sight of a snake was a rarity, there was no help then for the conviction that the next footstep would fall on a coiled rattler. An imaginary snake is so much more fearful than a real one, that I should rather handle a rattlesnake, as I have done since, than dream of one. I dreaded the sunset, thinking of the dark box of the outhouse.

Cross Creek, 59

Two male bears were moving slowly down the road. . . . They were on their hind legs, walking like men, shoulder to shoulder. Their walk seemed almost a dance, as when couples in the square dance moved side by side to do a figure. . . . Jody stood until the procession passed from sight, solemn and ludicrous and exciting.

The Yearling, 200–201

"I got to have he'p. My dogs is all right, but a big woman and a leetle man and a yearlin' boy is no match for that many hongry wolves huntin' in a pack."

Penny, *The Yearling*, 284

"When you ain't lookin' for a deer . . . they're all over the place. When you hunt 'em, you'd think you was in a tormented city."

Penny, *The Yearling*, 316

"Why, that's his goozle. What's a goozle? Well, if he didn't have no goozle, he couldn't squeal."

Ma, *The Yearling*, 274

Ants have played havoc with my belief that anything is interesting when known. Having come prepared to loathe crawling things and stayed to admire them, I came full of copy-book reverence for the ant and remain filled with the desire to exterminate the last one. In a still predatory world, good and evil are not fixed values, but are relative. "Good" is what helps us or at least does not hinder. "Evil" is whatever harms us or interferes with us, according to our own selfish standards. The ant as a symbol of industry, of social organization, of superb community instinct, has been extolled by science as well as the Bible. But for whom does the ant function so industriously and so socially? No one has troubled to point out that it is for the ant.

Cross Creek, 151

Rattlers got out of the way when they had a chance.

The Yearling, 169

The rattler struck [Penny] from under the grape-vine without warning. Jody saw the flash, blurred as a shadow, swifter than a martin, surer that the slashing claws of a bear. He saw his father stagger backward under the force of the blow. He heard him give a cry. He wanted to step back, too. He wanted to cry out with all his voice. He stood rooted to the sand and could not make a sound. . . . He saw the mottled shadow lift its flat head, knee-high. The head swung from side to side, following his father's slow motions. He heard the rattles hum. . . . As slowly as a man in a dream, Penny backed away. The rattles sung. . . . Penny lifted his gun to his shoulder and fired. Jody quivered. The rattler coiled and writhed in its spasms. The head was buried in the sand. The contortions moved down the length of the thick body, the rattles whirred feebly and were still. The coiling flattened into slow convolutions, like a low tide ebbing. Penny turned and stared at his son. . . . "He got me."

The Yearling, 145–46

"And here's a question my daddy allus asked and nobody couldn't never answer. Why do a soft-shell cooter lay a hard-shelled egg, and a hard-shelled cooter lay a soft-shelled egg?"

Mart, "Jacob's Ladder," *Short Stories*, 54

Old Jib has lived to be a veritable Egyptian mummy of a cat, lean and desiccated, with an eye cocked to watch the birds and the chameleons he has not disturbed for many years. Life will be for him always a lively matter, even when it is reduced to mere speculation.

Cross Creek, 33

"Now boy, tie up the creetur and fergit him. He ain't a dog, he ain't a young un, though you near about made one outen him. You cain't carry him places like a gal would a play-dolly."

Penny, *The Yearling*, 318

I never planned to shoot the pig and I certainly didn't know it belonged to Mr. Martin. As a matter of fact, I didn't care. It could have belonged to the devil himself, and many a morning I was sure of it. I am a patient woman as far as other people's stock is concerned. I know stock. If I were a pig, I should search out the green pastures, as did the pigs of Mr. Martin. If I knew where skimmed milk lay white and frothy in open pans, I should push my way under a stout barbed-wire fence and bury my snout in that milk. But even if I were a pig, I can see no reason for rooting up fluffy-ruffle petunias.

Cross Creek, 98

A varmint . . . is any one of the wild things in the woods either definitely predatory or of no domestic service. A human varmint is one who possesses skulking qualities and may be expected to be "low down." We use the epithets "bastard" and "son of a bitch" freely in these parts, and the former in particular is not a fighting term, but may even be used with a certain amount of affection.

Cross Creek, 156–57

Human Nature

Rawlings signs a copy of *Cross Creek* at Cohen Brothers Department Store in Jacksonville, Florida, December 1942. Photograph by Elsner Photo. Courtesy of the Department of Special and Area Studies Collections, George A. Smathers Libraries, University of Florida.

It's pure impudence to complain about much of ary thing, excusing human nature, and we all got a just complaint against that.

Quincey Dover, "Cocks Must Crow," *Short Stories*, 252

Man-nature is man-nature, and a woman's a fool to interfere. A man worth his salt can't be helt to heel like a bird dog. Give him his head. Leave him run. If he knows he ain't running under a checkrein, the devil hisself can't get him to run more'n about so far away from his regular rations. Men is the most regular creatures on earth. All they need is to know they can run if they want to. That satisfies them.

Quincey Dover, "Cocks Must Crow," *Short Stories*, 254

"You sly scaper. . . . You gittin' slick as a clay road in the rain."

Ma, *The Yearling*, 13

When we was fresh-married I said to him, "You're soft-acting, Will Dover, but you got a will as hard as a gopher shell."

Quincey Dover to Will,
"Cocks Must Crow," *Short Stories*, 254

"You ain't fooling me none, neither. . . . You got a tongue as sharp as a new cane knife, but your heart's as big as your behind, and soft as summer butter."

Will Dover to Quincey,
"Cocks Must Crow," *Short Stories*, 254

It's an awful thing when a woman has done builded her life on a man and she finds his legs is made of sand.

Quincey Dover, "Cocks Must Crow," *Short Stories*, 260

"Folks around here is techy if a man don't act friendly. They mighty good neighbors, if a man'll be friendly. Hit'd pleasure 'em consid'able, did we invite 'em to a break-down, time the house is mended and the new part built and things fixed nice."

Luke, *Golden Apples*, 174

"Most women folk cain't see for their lives, how a man loves so to ramble. . . . Men-folks has got to stick together in the name o' peace."

Penny, *The Yearling*, 10–11

Her pertness enchanted them. Young men went away from her with a feeling of bravado. Old men were enslaved by her silver curls. Something about her was forever female and made all men virile. Her gift infuriated all women.

The Yearling, 113–14

"A white woman don't ask another white woman to do her washin' for her, nor to carry her slops. . . . 'Course, in time o' sickness or trouble or sich as that a woman does ary thing she can for another and they's no talk o' pay."

Tim, *Cross Creek*, 67

"I been studyin'. A man kin love a woman a heap o' ways. He kin love her the way he love a drink o' likker on a cold evenin'. He kin love her hateful-like, the way a man that loves the taste o' quail-meat'll kill 'em in the nestin' season, jest so he gits the good of 'em hisself. Or he kin love her the way I'd be proud to figger you done loved Allie—gentle-like and lookin' out for her."

Luke, *Golden Apples*, 260

I'd tried to take his manhood from him, so he didn't have no way to strut but fighting a rooster. Now he'd won, and he was a man again. And I knowed that cocks must crow.

Quincey Dover, "Cocks Must Crow," 270

You can't change a man, no-ways. By the time his mammy turns him loose and he takes up with some innocent woman and marries her, he's what he is. If it's his nature to set by the hearth-fire and scratch hisself, you just as good to let him set and scratch.

Quincey Dover, "Benny and the Bird Dogs,"
Short Stories, 198

"I reckon we be as cur'ous to the creeturs as they be to us. . . . You kin tame a 'coon. You kin tame a bear. You kin tame a wild-cat and you kin tame a panther." He pondered. His mind went back to his father's sermons. "You kin tame arything, son, excusin' the human tongue."

Penny, *The Yearling*, 84–85

The technique was obvious and simple. When one went in, one placed the flag in the path. When one came out, one put the flag back inside the outhouse. One went in and put the flag in the path. One returned to the house, forgetting to put the flag back again. The flag stood like a red light against traffic, for hours and hours and hours.

Cross Creek, 59

"Hit's male nature, boy. Wait 'til you git to courtin' and you'll git your breeches dusted many a time."

Buck, *The Yearling*, 187

Something about the pelican's shadow, darkening her heart and mind with that absurd desperation, must be connected with some profound and secret dread, but she could not seem to put her finger on it.

"The Pelican's Shadow," *Short Stories*, 296

There were not many rags in the Baxter household. Clothes were worn and patched and mended until they dropped in ribbons. Flour sacks went into aprons and dish-towels and chair-backs that she embroidered on winter evenings; into backs for her patch-work quilts.

The Yearling, 181

Ase drove back to the farm with his only true though unbegotten son, their kinship not of the blood but of the spirit. The physical continuity of the generations bore little or no relation, he thought, to that kinship of mind that flashed its inexplicable recognition, one beacon signaling another across the darkness.

The Sojourner, 307

"I'd heap ruther a woman tore me down with a lighter'd knot, than speakin' sharp."

Buck, *The Yearling*, 189

The Negroes, who are infallible snobs, recognized the mark of high caste that illuminated his drunkenness and his violence and spoke of him always as Mister Marsh Turner.

Cross Creek, 140

She is illiterate, she can tell a judicious lie when necessary, she does not know sterling silver from aluminum, and scours old English Sheffield along with the cooking pots and pans. But she is well-bred. Breeding after all is a matter of manner, of social adjustment, of exquisite courtesy. Perhaps she is descended from old African kings and queens. At any rate, the hallmark is on her.

On Martha Mickens, *Cross Creek*, 25

I bought Georgia of her father for five dollars. The surest way to keep a maid at the Creek, my new friend told me, was to take over a very young Negro girl and train her in my ways. She should be preferably without home ties so that she should become attached to me. My friends traced a newly widowered father of a large family that he was unable to feed as a unit. He was happy to "give" me Georgia, with no strings attached. A five-dollar-bill sealed the bargain. Two months of life with her made me wonder why he had not given her to the first passing gypsy caravan, or drowned her decently. . . . No one knew her exact age, but it was somewhere between ten and twelve. At any rate, Georgia was unteachable. . . . I gave her father five dollars to take her back again.

Cross Creek, 77–79

I had always known that we were building up to this; that it was not she who was serving me, but I who was destined to serve her.

On 'Geechee, *Cross Creek*, 85

It was like being in the hands of a black Florence Nightingale. All of us, no matter how self-reliant, long, I think, for tenderness. Her big rough hands touched me as gently as though I were made of glass, instead of being almost as sturdy as she.

Cross Creek, 94

"Her and me don't never swop much honey."

Ma, *The Yearling*, 317

Sometimes there are friendships that have no apparent reason for existence, between people set apart by every circumstance of life, yet so firm in their foundations

that they survive conditions that would separate friends of more apparent suitability.

Cross Creek, 108

"The worst things I knows of is rattlesnakes and some kinds o' people. And a rattlesnake minds his own matters if he ain't bothered. A man's got a right to kill ary thing, snake or man, comes messin' up with him."

Lantry, *South Moon Under*, 7

I am not of the race of southerners who claim to understand the Negro. There are a few platitudes dear to the hearts of these that seem reasonably accurate. The Negro is just a child. The Negro is carefree and gay. The Negro is religious in an amusing way. The Negro is a congenital liar. There is no dependence to be put in the best of them. Back of these superficial truths lies the mystery of the primitive African nature, subjected precipitously first to slavery and then to so-called civilization, the one as difficult and unjust as the other.

Cross Creek, 180

One may usually spare one's breath in questioning a Negro about a theft, especially that of liquor. The slave status has made the lie a social necessity.

Cross Creek, 92

One's relations with Negroes are like love affairs. When they end, they end.

Cross Creek, 188–89

I am never done with marvelling at the sensitivity to beauty of presumably the dullest and most ignorant souls.

Cross Creek, 80

"I'm sorry. But that's the way I am. I go along quietly for a while, and then out of a clear sky I just don't know what I'm doing. I pick up a gun and I shoot whatever makes me angry. This time it was a pig. I'm so afraid some time it may be a person. After it was over, I'd be terribly sorry. But then it would be too late, wouldn't it?"

MKR to Mr. Martin, *Cross Creek*, 101

The word means something very special to me, and the quality for which I use it is a rare one. My father had it—there is another of whom I am almost sure—but almost no man of my acquaintance possesses it with the clarity, the purity, the simplicity of a mountain stream.

On integrity, "A Mother in Mannville,"
Short Stories, 245

15
· · · · · ·

Air

There was no breeze. The air lay over the road like a thick down comforter. It seemed to Jody that it was something that could be pushed away, if he could struggle up through it. The sand burned his bare calloused soles.

The Yearling, 143

The road went up an incline. At the top he stopped. The April sky was framed by the tawny sand and the pines. It was as blue as his homespun shirt, dyed with Grandma Hutto's indigo. Small clouds were stationary, like bolls of cotton. As he watched, the sunlight left the sky a moment and the clouds were gray.

The Yearling, 3

The wind rose as the three men sat at supper. There was an hour of gale, moving in from the southeast in short gusts. The palm fronds whipped violently. The hammock was riotous. The great oaks about the house vibrated, offering a solid bulk against the wind. The rain came in the darkness, sweeping in vast torrents. The shingled roof was a sounding board, and the rain drummed across it in a wild richness.

Golden Apples, 176

The girl was awakened by the tumult. It was broad day, and the outer perimeter of the hurricane was moving across the section. The yellow-grayness of the sky was tinged with green in the west. The roar of the wind was a train thundering nearer and nearer. The palmettos thrashed their fans in frenzy. Rain was pounding on the roof as though it would beat it open. On the gutters it flailed like bird-shot. The thunder no more than boomed above the down-pour. Beyond the kitchen window, the gray flood was a curtain across the piney-woods. The world outside the cabin was obliterated.

"Jacob's Ladder," *Short Stories*, 48

The afternoon sun was brilliant. The golden balls on the round trees flashed, as though their rinds were of some bright metal. From the hill-top, the sky was infinite; the thick blue of turquoises, solid and incredible. The evergreen leaves glinted like a dark jade. There was no wind. The trees stood motionless, no heavy branches stirring.

Golden Apples, 236

A breeze parted the canopied limbs over him. The sun dropped through and lay on his head and shoulders. It

was good to be warm at his head while his hard calloused feet were cold. The breeze died away, the sun
no longer reached him. He waded across to the op-
posite bank where the growth was more open. A low
palmetto brushed him. It reminded him ... that he had
planned as long ago as Christmas, to make himself a
flutter-mill.

The Yearling, 5

The breeze reached the bed and brushed him with the
cool softness of clean fur. He lay for a moment in torment between the luxury of his bed and the coming
day. Then he was out of his nest.

The Yearling, 23

They set off to the west. The sun was still above the
tree-tops. There had been no rain in several days, but
now cumulus clouds were piled low in the north and
west. From the east and south, a steel grayness crept
toward the glaring brilliance of the west.

The Yearling, 143

The wind was rising. [Jody] heard it far off in the distance. It was as though it were blowing in another
world, across a dark abyss. Suddenly it swelled. He
heard it coming closer, like a moving wall. The trees
ahead thrashed their limbs. The bushes rattled and flattened to the ground. There was a great roaring and the
storm hit him like a blow.

The Yearling, 153

The most engaging of bird flights to my notion is that of the red-birds. They seem to take life very lightly and in motion they give an effect of haphazard gayety. They seem not to fly of their own volition, but, scatterbrained, to be tossed from tree to tree like wind-blown leaves.

Cross Creek, 272

The wind blew in gusts down the chimney, a pleasant intruder, like the dog, who waited politely from the kitchen threshold for his own plate.

The Sojourner, 44

Jody put his arms under his head and looked up into the sky. It was as thick with stars as a pool of silver minnows. Between the two tall pines over him, the sky was milky, as though Trixie had kicked a great bucket of milk foaming across the heavens. The pines swayed back and forth in a light cool breeze. Their needles were washed with the silver of the starlight.

The Yearling, 255

Sorrow was like the wind. It came in gusts, shaking the woman.

South Moon Under, 77

The air, like that of delirium, was palpable, pressing on her bony shoulders an insupportable weight.

"Jacob's Ladder," *Short Stories*, 102

He was like the changing clouds and the setting sun and the rising moon. A part of him had been always outside his twisted body. It had come and gone like the wind. It came to Jody that he need not be lonely for his friend again. He could endure his going.

The Yearling, 219

The human mind scatters its interests as though made of thistle-down, and every wind stirs and moves it.

"A Mother in Mannville," *Short Stories*, 249

Jody felt uneasy and miserable, alone on the edge of the marsh. The world seemed empty. Only over the scrub the buzzards wheeled, profiting. . . . He climbed to the top of the load of hay and lay flat on his back, staring at the sky. He decided that the world was a very peculiar place to live in. Things happened that had no reason and made no sense and did harm, like the bears and panthers, but without their excuse of hunger. He did not approve.

The Yearling, 269

And after he had known all possible of this earth, he longed to know still others, to walk like a god the starry sky. The sky itself could scarcely satisfy, it was infinity for which he yearned, to be absorbed in it, never again lonely, the cosmos filtering through his conscious being, and he in turn returning to the cosmos his own awareness.

The Sojourner, 169

There was a breathless hush in the forest, but overhead gray clouds scudded wildly to the southwest. There was terror in the flight of these imponderable things, as though the forces pounding in behind them were those of a pestilence. The sky blackened moment by moment. Twilight took over the woods; then dark. There was no morning; no day; no longer any time.

"Jacob's Ladder," *Short Stories*, 104

Light and Darkness

The hammock stood stripped and naked. Where there had been darkness, there was light. The early sun streamed through the gray atmosphere and settled in the newly opened spaces as into a valley. It hung there, tasting soil it had never touched before.

Golden Apples, 164

Darkness filled both land and water. A hoot owl cried in the thicket near him. He shivered. The night wind stirred and was chill. He heard a rustling that might be leaves moving ahead of the wind, or small creatures passing. He was not afraid.

The Yearling, 415-16

The orchard was probed by a rosy light, was abandoned by it. The twilight was the blue of the hickory smoke. Then it too drifted across the valley, trailed over the hilltops and was gone. There was a time of dusk that was never darkness. The men threw themselves on their backs in the soft grass and stared at the night sky. Stars were tangled in the apple branches.

The Sojourner, 115

The blood-red bands across the west dissolved one into the other. The color settled to the rim of the horizon, coagulating. A layer of red-gold washed the lower trunks of the pine trees. For a moment it lay in a stain about their feet. Then it faded and was gone. There was an instant's gray light that was neither night nor day. It too was gone and the pine-woods were black and solid. The walkers moved closer to the road, to be guided by the light of its pale sand.

Golden Apples, 191

There was no light but the endless flickering of stars. She knew that if the man did not come back again she would have to follow him. Solitude she had endured. She could not endure desolation.

"Gal Young Un," *Short Stories*, 158

All year the orange grove is luminous. The oleanders glisten. The palm trees shed the cold as blandly as the rain. Unless severe frost has struck them, the Turk's-cap and hibiscus bear red lanterns day in, day out, to light the timid before the dark face of time. Only the pecan trees scattered through the grove shed their leaves in November and stand stripped and shivering until April.

Cross Creek, 243–44

The sun set molten, beneficence gone mad. The evening was a soft gray velvet suffocation.

"Jacob's Ladder," *Short Stories*, 98

Jody opened his eyes unwillingly. . . . The daylight lay in orange streaks. The pines beyond the clearing were still black against it. Now in April the sun was rising earlier. . . . The bright streaks in the east thickened and blended. A golden flush spread as high as the pines, and as he watched, the sun itself lifted, like a vast copper skillet being drawn to hang among the branches.

The Yearling, 22–23

Hurricanes are not a serious menace in the interior, but we get the fringes of the big coastal storms. An ominous green light precedes them, and a great stillness that may hold for twenty-four hours. The green deepens, is infiltrated with a cosmic black ink, and the skywriting has its plain meaning. Then in the distance we hear a roaring, as though the express passing through the village had left its tracks and were headed for the Creek.

Cross Creek, 305–6

The hammock was no longer quite dark. There was no visible light, yet the forest was luminous. Live oaks detached themselves from the blackness and lifted great boughs against the light. Palms cut sharply into the brighter air. The moon lunged out of the eastern edge of the hammock and hung a moment before rising farther. It was a few days past the full and its silver was a little tarnished. It lifted slowly, the metallic disc warped at one side, and crooked.

Golden Apples, 197

Night entered the clearing from the scrub. The low tangled growth of young oak and pine and palmetto fell suddenly black and silent, seeming to move closer in one shadowy spring. The man told himself there was nothing to fear. Yet as he walked towards his cabin, naked and new on the raw sand, darkness in this place seemed to him unfriendly.

South Moon Under, 1

He stretched out one arm and laid his head on it. A shaft of sunlight, warm and thin like a light patchwork quilt, lay across his body. He watched the flutter-mill indolently, sunk in the sand and the sunlight. The movement was hypnotic. His eyelids fluttered with the palm-leaf paddles. Drops of silver slipping from the wheel blurred together like the tail of a shooting star. The water made a sound like kittens lapping. . . . The blue, white-tufted sky closed over him. He slept.

The Yearling, 6

Time

Time for him was not marked off in jumps, as Nellie expressed it. It was not clearly marked and definite, it was all one, sometimes relative but forever whole. All life seemed to him contained in the beginning and the end, if there had ever been a beginning and if there would ever be an end. Time was, must be, timeless. As from a great enough height a landscape would show no detail, so from a far enough distance all time would be seen to exist simultaneously. He felt this in his inner mind and spirit.

The Sojourner, 159

I got nothing particular against time. Time's a natural thing. Folks is a kind of accident on the face of the earth, but time was here before us. And when we've done finished messing ourselves up, and when the last man turns over to die, saying, "Now how come us to make such a loblolly of living?"—why, time'll rock right on.

Quincey Dover, "Cocks Must Crow," *Short Stories*, 252

Rawlings and Cal Long on the set of *The Yearling*, 1945. Long was the source for the story of Jody and Flag in *The Yearling* and the model for "Old Man Paine" in *South Moon Under*. Courtesy of the Department of Special and Area Studies Collections, George A. Smathers Libraries, University of Florida.

The sign was unexpected, and I was suddenly lost in a wave of timelessness. I thought for an instant that I was back in the May of a year ago. Then it seemed to me that I had skipped this present season and had been precipitated into the coming year. The pecan tree was bearing again, and where was I in time and space? And the old comfort came, in the recurrence, and on the heels of the comfort, despair, that there was no end to seasons, but an end to me.

Cross Creek, 244

Time ain't got the decency of a rattlesnake. A rattler most times'll give warning.

Quincey Dover, "Cocks Must Crow," *Short Stories*, 253

[T]ime's a low-down, sneaking, cottonmouth moccasin, drops its fangs without you knowing it's even in the grass, and was there ary thing I could do about it, I'd do it. Excusing that, I got nothing against time.

Quincey Dover, "Cocks Must Crow," 253

He wondered if he could explain his sense of timelessness. He did not think of it as another life, nor yet quite an immortality of the same one. It was only, he felt, that individual lives could no more be separated from life itself than drops of water from the mass of ocean. He was willing to give to life the name of "God," since men knew no other large enough with which to speak of the ineffable, the Word made Life. He supposed men were not yet fit or ready to be entrusted, desperately as they needed it, with the secret of the Word. No, he could not explain.

The Sojourner, 283

Religion

The church at Cross Creek. Courtesy of the Department of Special and Area Studies Collections, George A. Smathers Libraries, University of Florida.

Martha is a Primitive, or foot-washing, Baptist, militant and certain of her doctrines.

Cross Creek, 26

"They's no end to what a man'll fight for. I even knowed a preacher takened off his coat and fit ary man wouldn't agree to infant damnation. All a feller kin do, is fight for what he figgers is right, and the devil take the hindmost."

Penny, *The Yearling*, 187

Man's law is one thing, God's another.

Cross Creek, 140

"I don't fish on Sundays. . . . I wa'n't raised up that-a-way."

Grampa Hicks, *Cross Creek*, 140

"Now I never had nothin' much to pet nor play with, neither. . . . There was sich a mess of us. Neither farmin' nor the Bible pays a man too good, and Pa was like your Ma, he jest wouldn't feed no creeturs. He done well to fill our bellies."

Penny, *The Yearling*, 103

"The devil gits blamed for a heap o' things is nothin' but human cussedness."

Penny, *The Yearling*, 199

Her feeling was, simply, that God knows best. What she meant by "God" I do not know, and no two people mean the same thing in their invocation of the mystic

Word. My own idea is that those of us who are least positive are closest to the truth. We know only that as human beings we are very stupid and that somewhere beyond us are forces unintelligibly wiser or cleverer or more fixed than we are. The forces may concern themselves with us or they may not, but it seems to me, and seemed to Widow Slater, that people live or die, thrive or pine, quite beyond human reason.

Cross Creek, 70

"I been in a heap o' churches. There's the Nazarene Church and the Pentecost and the Holy Rollers and the Baptists and I don't know what-all. I cain't see much difference to nary one of 'em. There's a good to all of 'em and there's a bad."

Abner, *South Moon Under*, 306

"I've heerd tell o' them, seems to me, . . . but I cain't rightly place 'em. Who was them Muslems? A form o' Catholics?"

"I cain't say as to that. But they pays right smart attention to the sun and figgers ever'thing comes fum the East, like. They think it's fitten and proper a man should keep hisself a hull mess o' wives."

"Seems to me that's all right."

Lonny, Abner, and Martin on "Muslems,"
South Moon Under, 306

"Now if I knowed they'd feed you this good in Heaven, I'd not holler when I die."

Buck, *The Yearling*, 251

A father at table should join himself to the others, whatever his private concerns. The breaking of bread together, the sharing of salt, the eating of meat, was a sacred thing, one small community against the outer darkness.

The Sojourner, 192

"Now I don't want to go to Heaven."
"Reckon there's no danger."

Grandma Hutto and Ma, *The Yearling*, 323

"One thing, the company I'd have to keep. . . . Another thing's the music. There's nothin' played there, they claim, but harps. Now the only music I like is a flute and a bass viol and an octave harp. Unless one o' your preachers'll guarantee that, I'll jest refuse the trip with thanks. . . . Another thing's the food. Even the Lord likes the incense of roasted meat before him. But accordin' to the preachers, folks in Heaven live on milk and honey. I despise milk and honey makes me sick to my stummick. . . . I figger Heaven's only folks' longin' for what they ain't had on earth. Well, I've had near about ever' thing a woman would want. Mebbe that's why I've got no interest."

Grandma Hutto to Jody on why she does not
wish to go to Heaven, *The Yearling*, 324

"A person allus gets out of life what he's entitled to. The Lord sees to that."

Widow Slater, *Cross Creek*, 76

I have my own explanation of the cynical Biblical statement that it is as easy for a rich man to enter Heaven as for a camel to pass through the eye of a needle. On the surface, the statement is unjust, for wealth is so accidental a thing, that either its possession or its lack should not be held against any man. . . . The rich, the well-favored, the well-situated, are surrounded with a confusing protective mass of extraneous and irrelevant matter that tends to hide the substance beneath. The poor, the unfortunate, have been put through the sieve and stand nakedly for what they are. A poor and simple man stands with bare outstretched hands at the gates of Heaven, for his essential character is written in broad letters across him, for life has stripped him down to it.

Cross Creek, 122–23

"You belong to be skeert, a'right. There ain't nothin' left to try. There ain't no'eres left to go. Us been a-climbin' ol' Jacob's ladder thouten no end to it."

Mart, "Jacob's Ladder," *Short Stories*, 100

There's no woman in the State of Florida has got more patience with the varmint in a man than me. It's in his blood, just like a woman has got a little snake and a mite of cat. A man's borned varminty and he dies varminty, and when the preacher asks do we believe our great-great-granddaddies was monkeys, I can't scarcely keep from standing up and saying, "Brother, a good ways back, I figure things was a heap worse mixed up than monkeys."

Quincey Dover, "Varmints," *Short Stories*, 226

"God takes care of fools and children."

Ed Hopkins on MKR's "discovery"
of a coral snake, *Cross Creek*, 168

He, too, he recognized, had sought to find the unfindable. He had lost and sought a brother, and it was in the faces of all men he should have peered. He had been homeless, and knew that for such men as he there was no home, only an endless journey. He had sought to know the unknowable. He and his whole race, great, slow, groping, God-touched children, would have to wait a long time, he supposed, for that, learning one lesson a millennium, sometimes forgetting it and having to begin all over. He himself, he thought humbly, had learned far too little. He had done much harm. He had known good from evil, and he had sat miserable and mute when the fight was called for. He had carried his standards into battle perhaps not quite too late. He could not know whether his good had been greater than his evil. No man could balance the delicate scales, for he himself weighted one end and could not reach across to weight the other. An invisible hand would add or subtract. An unheard voice would speak the answer.

The Sojourner, 325–26

Being busy with the checking of admissions to Heaven, it is conceivable that St. Peter is obliged to tell the rich man that he must wait in the anteroom until he can go deeper into his case.

Cross Creek, 123

"Oh Lord. Almighty God. Hit ain't for us ignorant mortals to say what's right and what's wrong. Was ary one of us to be a-doin' of it, we'd not of brung this pore boy into the world a cripple, and his mind teched. We'd of brung him in straight and tall like his brothers, fitten to live and work and do. But in a way o' speakin', Lord, you done made it up to him. You give him a way with the wild creeturs. You give him a sort o' wisdom, made him knowin' and gentle. The birds come to him, and the varmints moved free about him, and like as not he could o' takened a she wild-cat right in his pore twisted hands. Now you've done seed fit to take him where bein' crookedy in mind or limb don't matter. But Lord, hit pleasures us to think now you've done straightened out them legs and that pore bent back and them hands. Hit pleasures us to think on him, movin' around as easy as ary one. And Lord, give him a few red-birds and mebbe a squirrel and a 'coon and a 'possum to keep him comp'ny, like he had here. All of us is somehow lonesome, and we know he'll not be lonesome, do he have them leetle wild things around him, if it ain't askin' too much to put a few varmints in Heaven. Thy will be done. Amen."

Penny's prayer for Fodder-wing, *The Yearling*, 211–12

Yet when a wave of love takes over a human being, love of another human being, love of nature, love of all mankind, love of the universe, such an exultation takes him that he knows he has put his finger on the pulse of the great secret and the great answer.

Cross Creek, 365

Tale-Telling

Rawlings presents her lunar side for her brother, Arthur H. Kinnan. Courtesy of the Department of Special and Area Studies Collections, George A. Smathers Libraries, University of Florida.

I have used a factual background for most of my tales, and of actual people a blend of the true and the imagined. I myself cannot quite tell where one ends and the other begins.

Cross Creek, 64

I ain't like them story writers can make a tale come out as even as a first-prize patchwork quilt. Life ain't slick like a story, no-ways. I got to remember this, and remember that, and when I'm done it'll makes sense.

Quincey Dover, "Cocks Must Crow," *Short Stories*, 256

It was good to become old and see the sights and hear the sounds that mean saw and heard, like Buck and his father. . . . They had seen marvels, and the older they were, the more marvels they had seen. He felt himself moving into a mystic company. He had a tale now of his own to tell on winter evenings.

The Yearling, 201

A Reader's Club, in advertising its wares, advises one and all to turn to books when love and liquor fail them. Love and liquor are admittedly fallible comforters, but who is to agree on books? One man's meat is another man's poison more certainly in literature than in gastronomy. Conversation is fallible, for not all want to

talk about the same things, and some do not want to talk at all, and some do not want to listen. But short of dyspepsia or stomach ulcers, any man or woman may be pleased with well-cooked and imaginative dishes.

Cross Creek, 205

Cookery is my one vanity and I am a slave to any guest who praises my culinary art. This is my Achilles heel. Dorothy Parker has a delightful verse dealing with the abuse she is willing to take from her beloved, and ending, "But say my verses do not scan, and I get me another man." For my part, my literary ability may safely be questioned as harshly as one wills, but indifference to my table puts me in a rage.

Cross Creek, 205–6

The Negro imagination is dark and rich. As they grow older, they learn to save it for their own kind, to hide it from unfriendly minds, perhaps, in an alien civilization. But a Negro child will some day make a sad and lovely study for a poet.

Cross Creek, 81

He sobbed and held on. A few inches at a time, he heaved the body across the gunwhales and into the boat. The big bull was all of twenty feet. The tail hung over the end. He paddled up the river, home. He left the 'gator in the boat, mooring it high among the cypress knees. He stumbled through the dark hammock; panting, into his bed.

South Moon Under, 184, second printing
(In the first printing, the "big bull" was "all of thirty feet.")

"'Gators is a mess. And a pain. I run over one last night.
I'd been out to Lobkirk's for a snort, and coming back
by Gopher Creek I saw the knocker climbing out of the
ditch to cross the road to water. I shot the juice to the
Model-T and I hit him just the time he got his head
over the rut. When he rared up, he carried the front
wheels of the car plumb over in the ditch. Model-T
shook loose, but before it got shut of him, he had me
going in the creek. I don't fancy 'em."

Fred, "Alligators," *Short Stories*, 184

On the chest of drawers were two books. One was the
Sears Roebuck catalogue, a hefty volume. I heaved it at
the moccasin. It hurt him enough so that he went into
convulsive coils instead of slipping under the bathtub
and I knew I could approach closer. The other book was
a copy of one of my own writings, *The Yearling*. I took
it and finished off the moccasin. I told Little Will next
morning of the encounter, and the method by which I
had dispatched the intruder. He chuckled. "It sho' do
come in handy to write books," he said.

Cross Creek, 178–79

Winter

We have one fixed seasonal dividing line. While spring and summer and fall merge silently one into the other, we announce winter with the crackling of gunshot.

Cross Creek, 311

The earth was stricken. The out-cropping granite in the bare pasture was the bones of the earth gnawed clean by the wolfish winds. Maples and oaks, hickories and willows were shivering skeletons. Pines and hemlocks were black and ominous against the gray November sky. Crows stretched evil wings on the ridge-pole of the sheep-shed, waiting for a lamb to die. No snow had fallen to hide the nakedness of the year's old age. The sprouts of young winter wheat shrank in the cold, would die if not soon covered with the white protective blanket.

The Sojourner, 139

The orphanage is high in the Carolina mountains. Sometimes in the winter the snow-drifts are so deep that the institution is cut off from the village below, from all the world. Fog hides the mountain peaks, the snow swirls down the valleys, and wind blows so bitterly that the orphanage boys who take the milk twice daily to the baby cottage reach the door with fingers still in an agony of numbness.

"A Mother in Mannville," *Short Stories*, 243

"Cold weather pleasures me consid'able. I shore hates to sweat into my fiddle."

Waverly the fiddler, *Golden Apples*, 181

Once upon a time there was snow at Cross Creek. The Chamber of Commerce would insist that this was not a factual item, but the beginning of a fairy tale.

Cross Creek, 322–23

"Snow's a searchin' thing. . . . Snow be's like sorrow. It searches people out."

Martha Mickens, *Cross Creek*, 323;
Martha, "Jacob's Ladder," *Short Stories,* 68

The December sun filled the earth with a thin filtered gold, without warmth. The palmetto fronds were metallic with its chill brightness. Out of the sun, the wind was cold.

Golden Apples, 187

The earth was thirsty for snow. The winter wheat, in peril of its life, shrank in need to be covered with the soft white blanket. The snow began falling at dusk from a still and milky sky. The flakes at first were large and loose. They slapped against walls, against the boughs and trunks of trees, with the wet impact of a child's kiss. They clung, slipped, melted, and the earth for an hour or more drank them in like rain. With the sudden dark, the air turned cold, the ground stiffened, the snow gathered itself together in compact crystals and fell hard and fast, as though the elements had had enough of softness. The sharp particles hissed against the window-panes, then settled down to a steady pelting.

The Sojourner, 76

Snow fell softly all the winter day. The world was an inverted paper weight, the snow filled the round atmosphere, it was the atmosphere itself, shredded into these cool white patterns. Layer on layer piled on the tree limbs, extended like arms for garments, so that the trees were dressed and shapely. The roofs of houses and barns and sheds were inches deep in eiderdown.

The Sojourner, 170

He was stabbed with the candle-light inside the safe comfort of the cabin; with the moonlight around it. He pictured old Slewfoot, the great black outlaw bear with one toe missing, rearing up in his winter bed and tasting the soft air and smelling the moonlight, as he, Jody, smelled and tasted them.

The Yearling, 14

"And lo, the angel of the Lord came upon them, and the glory of the Lord shone round about them: and they were sore afraid." As always, the majestic language moved him; the talk of shepherds, abiding in the field.

Luke 2:9, *The Sojourner*, 97

Christmas is celebrated quietly at the Creek. None of the holidays has the festival air of the north. . . . We have no need of the emotional outlet of specified gala occasions. Thanksgiving is only a name.

Cross Creek, 327

There had been nothing special for Christmas the year before except a wild turkey for dinner because there had been no money. This year there was the money left from the sale of the bear cubs. Penny set aside a portion for cotton-seed and said the rest might be spent for Christmas.

The Yearling, 315

"Now if we goin to the doin's, I want to go tradin' to Volusia 'fore then. I want me four yards o' alpacy so I kin have Christmas decent."

Ma, *The Yearling*, 315

Christmas day was clear and sparkling. The sun gathered its strength. The icicles were struck to the heart, wept long crystal tears, lost their grip on their week-long home under the eaves, fell tinkling and broken to the ground.

The Sojourner, 99

At Christmas time I thought of the man's baggy clothes, his still uncut hair, his quicksilver and his dejection, and made up a box for him; a cooked ham, a fruit cake, pecans and candy.

Cross Creek, 129–30

A blizzard swept south into Florida at the end of December. Ice-filled winds lashed the state far below the orange belt. The gales reached a velocity of thirty miles an hour. During three days the temperature dropped lower and lower, until on the twenty-ninth, the thermometer stood at fourteen degrees above zero. Small ponds, that had been lush with tropical growth, were solid with ice. Warm, turgid lakes were frozen far out from the shore-line. The rank vegetation was cut down with a frigid scythe. The orange trees shrank within themselves, resisting. The fruit itself was frozen. The human inhabitants, wanton of habit as to the weather, huddled over ineffectual hearth fires.

Golden Apples, 281

The January weather was mild. Now and then the sun would set in a cold red stillness, quilts would be inadequate through the night, and morning would show a thin film of ice on the water buckets. Then in a day or two it would be so warm that Ma Baxter could sit on the porch in the sun in the afternoon and work at her mending and patching, and Jody could run through the woods without his wool jacket.

The Yearling, 371

"You men have just eaten a typical Yankee Christmas dinner. Now tell me, what is the usual Cracker Christmas dinner?" . . . "Whatever we can git, Ma'am . . . Whatever we can git."

MKR's question and Moe Sykes's response, *Cross Creek*, 110

One late winter day in my first year I discovered under the palm tree by the gate a small pile of Amaryllis bulbs. The yard was desperate for flowers and greenery and I began separating the bulbs to set out for spring blooming. I dug with my fingers under the pile and brought out in my hand not a snake, surely, but a ten-inch long piece of Chinese lacquer. The slim inert reptile was an exquisite series of shining bands of yellow and black and vermillion, with a tiny black nose. I thought, "Here is a snake, in my hands, and it is beautiful as a necklace."

MKR finds a coral snake, *Cross Creek*, 168

Philosophy

Thoreau went off to live in the woods alone, to find out what the world was like. Now a man may learn a deal of the general from studying the specific, whereas it is impossible to know the specific by studying the general. For that reason, our philosophers are usually the most impractical of men, while very simple folk may have a great deal of wisdom.

Cross Creek, 359

I do not know the irreducible minimum of happiness for any other spirit than my own. It is impossible to be certain even of mine. Yet I believe that I know my tangible desideratum. It is a tree-top against a patch of sky.

Cross Creek, 28

It seems strange, the way in maturity one sometimes recalls from childhood a long-forgotten incident, or chain of incidents, and finds the memory flooded with a brilliant light of understanding. It is as though one comes across a box of old playthings in the attic, among them a lump of modeling clay half formed into a figure, and one moistens the clay again and the proper shape comes at once, as the child could not have managed it years before. Or as though one reads a book that had been read without comprehension when young, and it is now, of course, crystal-clear.

"Miriam's Houses," *Short Stories*, 352

We listen hopefully for the big bull alligator in Orange Lake, prophesying change.

Cross Creek, 299

Any grove or any wood is a fine thing to see. But the magic here, strangely, is not apparent from the road. It is necessary to leave the impersonal highway, to step inside the rusty gate and close it behind. By this, an act of faith is committed, through which one accepts blindly the communion cup of beauty. One is now inside the grove, out of one world and in the mysterious heart of another. Enchantment lies in different things for each of us. For me, it is in this: to step out of the bright sunlight into the shade of orange trees; to walk under the arched canopy of their jadelike leaves; to see

the long aisles of lichened trunks stretch ahead in geometric rhythm; to feel the mystery of a seclusion that yet has shafts of light striking through it. This is the essence of an ancient and secret magic. . . . And after long years of spiritual homelessness, of nostalgia, here is that mystic loveliness of childhood again. Here is home. An old thread, long tangled, comes straight again.

Cross Creek, 7–8

"And what should I do without hardness? The soft go down. Soft women—they go down."

Camilla, *Golden Apples*, 242

There is a healthy challenge in danger and a certain spiritual sustenance comes from fighting it.

Cross Creek, 332

Old Aunt Martha Mickens, with her deceptive humility and her face like poured chocolate, is perhaps the shuttle that has woven our knowledge, carrying back and forth, with the apparent innocence of a nest-building bird, the most revealing bits of gossip; the sort of gossip that tells, not trivial facts, but human motives and the secrets of human hearts. Each of us pretends that she carries these threads only about others and never about us, but we all know better, and that none of us is spared.

Cross Creek, 5

The road seemed simple enough. It was even pleasant, for to comfort any mortal against loneliness, one other is enough.

Golden Apples, 16

Her mischievous vitality had no place in his theories or his philosophy. She would reject the outer cosmic spaces, as she had rejected all thought of immortality of body or of spirit, the one life, she had said jestingly, having almost killed her. Yet surely she was not lost entirely. Something of her would breathe with the lilacs, would give delight to other lovers on other windy springtime hills.

The Sojourner, 297

Ghosts take a great responsibility when they encourage mortals.

Cross Creek, 129

It is more important to live the life one wishes to live, and to go down with it if necessary, quite contentedly, than to live more profitably but less happily. Yet to achieve content under sometimes adverse circumstances, requires first an adjustment within oneself, . . . and after that, a recognition that one is not unique in being obliged to toil and struggle and suffer. This is the simplest of all facts and the most difficult for the individual ego to accept.

Cross Creek, 19

Fearlessness was her defense against the world. She was conscious neither of happiness nor of unhappiness. She accepted.

On Florry, "Jacob's Ladder," *Short Stories*, 45

Callousness, I think, is often ignorance, rather than cruelty.

Cross Creek, 66

A man's thoughts, a man's dreams—Why, they were thoughts and dreams, and there was a long bridge between them and the world of fact.

"The Provider," *Short Stories*, 337

Four years in jail will surely do something to a man's initiative.

On Leroy, *Cross Creek*, 87

We lonely humans need very little of devotion for contentment.

Cross Creek, 89

"None of us don't never know what we want 'til it's mebbe too late to git it."

Nellie, *The Yearling*, 347

It makes one very humble to receive a forgiveness one does not deserve.

Cross Creek, 363

The human ego is a fearful thing and we consider those things, friends, relatives, stock, that touch our lives, to be somehow different because they are close to us.

Cross Creek, 250

People with a philosophy are usually inconsistent.

Cross Creek, 70

Water

A spring as clear as well water bubbled up from no-where in the sand. It was as though the banks cupped green leafy hands to hold it. There was a whirlpool where the water rose from the earth. Grains of sand boiled in it. Beyond the bank, the parent spring bub-bled up at a higher level, cut itself a channel through white limestone and began to run rapidly down-hill to make a creek. The creek joined Lake George, Lake George was a part of the St. John's River, the great river flowed northward and into the sea. It excited Jody to watch the beginning of the ocean. There were other be-ginnings, true, but this one was his own.

The Yearling, 4

A drizzle of rain fell in the February morning. The be-neficence of sun was gone.

Golden Apples, 298

The dusky glen laid cool hands on him. He rolled up the hems of his blue denim breeches and stepped with bare dirty feet into the shallow spring. . . . The water was so cold that for a moment it burned his skin. Then it made a rippling sound, flowing past his pipe-stem legs, and was entirely delicious.

The Yearling, 4

The boat, the river, the lake, had seemed transfixed in space, pendulous in the fog between the eternities of the past and the eternities of the future. He had a sense of stepping now into unreality, as though all of the American Florida were a dream; as though in it he passed into a life that was beyond life.

Golden Apples, 36

The River Styx was broad with its periodic overflow. Normally a trickle of current through vast miles of marsh, unseasonable rains had raised it until the narrow stream merged with the marsh waters, and river and marsh were one. The broad expanse of waters was copper-colored in the sun. The flat pads of water lilies lay in clusters and arrowhead lilies lifted white spears of bloom. Floating tussocks were alive with soldier blackbirds and rice birds. Their din filled the air, shrill and tuneless.

Golden Apples, 38

The scrub rolled towards its boundaries like a dark sea. It cast itself against the narrow beach of swamp and hammock that fringed the rivers. The two types of growth did not mingle, as though an ascetic race withdrew itself from a tropical one and refused to interbreed. The moisture along the rivers gave a footing for the lush growth of cypress in the swamp; of live oak, magnolia, hickory, ash, bay, sweet gum and holly that made up the adjoining hammock.

South Moon Under, 3

The lake was blue cobalt in the bright morning. The sunlight flecked the ripples with gold. The green bonnets extended in layers far out into the lake. They were shining and metallic, lifting as the waves lifted. The brisk breeze was off-shore and within the lee of the hammock the water was not too rough for comfort.

Golden Apples, 140

They reached the St. John's River. It was dark and aloof. It seemed to slide toward the ocean indifferent to its own banks and to the men who crossed or used it. Jody stared at it. It was a pathway to the world.

The Yearling, 109

Over his shoulder, closing the door, the cabin stood in the clearing like a house on an island. He thought that he heard the river running below the ledge. The river was a wall for his back. In front of the clearing the scrub rolled in, lapping at the edges of the bare sand like a vast sea.

South Moon Under, 10

A freight steamer was thrashing up-stream. He heard the side-wheel paddles drinking the swift current of the river. They gulped great wet mouthfuls and let it spill out again.

The Yearling, 132

Dead limbs were falling in the swamp. It was a certain sign of rain. They fell from the trees before and after, as though some dropped in terror of the moist burden, and others resisted a little longer. Limpkins were crying, and it would not be long before the grey curtain over the scrub and river dissolved into a sweep of rain. A drop spattered now and then like lead on a palmetto leaf.

South Moon Under, 291

We finished the scanty counting along Orange Lake and cut west toward the River Styx. The name chilled me. My mare was obstreperous, and as we moved into a wet narrow road, I thought that all that was needed to make her bolt under me was the sight of a moccasin. As though I had conjured him up, he was there. We were approaching a wooden foot-bridge and the mare, who had balked at all previous bridges, was taking this one of her own accord. The snake lay on a mound of earth to the right of the bridge. He was solidly coiled, an ancestral cottonmouth, taking up as much space as a dishpan. His triangular and venomous head rested flatly on the outer edge of his coils. The mare failed to see him because he lay so still. She was intent on her footing, on the welcome sight of the road ahead. Her careful, dainty hooves passed three inches from the dark sleek head. I loosened my feet from the stirrups, ready to jump free. The patriarch eyed me and did not stir. I decided that such a live-and-let-live philosophy was admirable, and I touched one finger to my hat, saluting a gentleman.

Cross Creek, 49–50

"You don't need to fear being caught in that stretch of swamp. . . . Nobody but Christ would try to walk it."

"One of the men," "Cracker Chidlings," *Short Stories*, 33

The east bank of the road shelved suddenly. It dropped below him twenty feet to a spring. The bank was dense with magnolia and loblolly bay, sweet gum and graybarked ash. He went down to the spring in the cool darkness of their shadows. A sharp pleasure came over him. This was a secret and a lovely place.

The Yearling, 4

The Silver River is as beautiful as its name. Dreamlike, it has an invisible source, rising from underground caverns to form Silver Springs, then flowing off into the sparsely populated Cracker hinterland east of Ocala. Like most lovely things, it has caused much squabbling among men.

"Cracker Chidlings," *Short Stories*, 39

In life every river had two banks, every sea two shores, and it was the privilege of living that a man might cross back and forth as long as the courage was in him.

Golden Apples, 349

The river flowed deep and dark. It made a rippling sound against the banks, but the great liquid heart of it moved silently. Only the swift progress of fallen leaves showed the current.

The Yearling, 115

"Ain't you noticed there's always cypress ponds in a flat woods? The 'gators travels in from the lakes and creeks to them and build theirselves caves. Like a gopher hole, only bigger. They dig 'em in the pond bank, under the water. A 'gator cave's about three feet across and anywhere from six to fifteen feet deep, according to the 'gator's size and notions. He generally likes to holler it out so he can roll over in it. A 'gator's the very devil for rolling."

Fred, "Alligators," *Short Stories*, 185

A scarcity of water was the only draw-back to the location. The water level lay so deep that wells were priceless. Water for inhabitants of Baxter's Island must come, until brick and mortal were cheaper, from the great sink-hole on the western boundary of the hundred-acre tract. The sink-hole was a phenomenon common to the Florida limestone regions. Underground rivers ran through such sections. The bubbling springs that turned at once into creeks and runs were outbreaks of these. Sometimes a thin shell of surface soil caved in and a great cavern was revealed, with or without a flow of water. The sink-hole included with Penny Baxter's land contained, unfortunately, no flowing spring. But a pure filtered water seeped day and night through the high banks and formed a pool at the bottom.

The Yearling, 19

"Flood or no flood, this is fine. I want you fellers to promise me one thing. When I'm an old man, set me on a stump and leave me listen to the hunt."

Penny, *The Yearling*, 252

The creek was a dark, lovely dream leading to the bright open of another world. The hammock pressed close on either side. Sometimes the rowboat scraped against cypress knees. Sometimes the moss-hung boughs of a live oak brushed like hands across it.

"Jacob's Ladder," *Short Stories*, 60

They had picked up the old Spanish trail through the hammock to Juniper Spring. The spring was at its normal level. Debris from the flood was thick about its banks. The spring itself bubbled clear and blue from a bottomless cavern.

The Yearling, 302

The wind had been high overhead. The rain was a solid wall, from sky to earth.

The Yearling, 224–25

He seemed to stand alone on a desolate shore while the tide went out. He was stranded there, no ship to bear him to sea, no horse to bear him inland. The wind keened high overhead and then was gone, passing trackless toward the uncharted stars.

The Sojourner, 260

The hammock merged into cypress swamp. A trumpet vine dropped flamboyant flowers from a lone palm. The blossoms seemed gaudy and funereal. There were no birds singing from the cypresses. No squirrels swung in and out of the sepulchral arches of the trees. Out of the dimly defined road a great white bird rose, flapping noiseless wings. It was huge, snow-white as an angel of death, with a wide black mourning band around the edge of the wings. I became aware that the soft dampness of the road had turned into a soft rippling. The whole floor of the forest was carpeted with amber-colored water, alive, moving with a slow, insidious current. We had entered the River Styx.

Cross Creek, 50–51

"Two women alone? The river runs through some of the wildest country in Florida. You'll be lost in the false channels. No one ever goes as far as the head of the river. . . . It will be splendid. What if you do get lost? Don't let anyone talk you out of it."

Contradictory male warning
on floating the St. Johns, *Cross Creek*, 343

"The river life's the finest kind of life. You couldn't get you no better than the river life."

Fisherman's wife, *Cross Creek*, 344

The river integrated itself again. The flat golden banks closed in on both sides of us, securing a snug safety. The strangeness of flowing water was gone, for it was all there was of living.

Cross Creek, 347

The mouth of the river was an end and beginning. At a certain point it could be said, "Here, now, the river is alive." A few yards more, past the last wind-beaten cedar, there was no longer any river. There was only the blue horizon. As it is told of a departing life, the river was not ended, but was become part of the sea's infinity.

"Jacob's Ladder," *Short Stories*, 79

The river resumed its broad quiet way as though it had left no tumult behind it. It had the dignity of age, was not now in that dark hurry to reach the sea. . . . I

thought in a panic, I shall never be happy on land again. I was afraid once more of all the painful circumstance of living. But when the dry ground was under us, the world no longer fluid, I found a forgotten loveliness in all the things that have nothing to do with men. Beauty is pervasive, and fills, like perfume, more than the object that contains it. Because I had known intimately a river, the earth pulsed under me. The Creek was home. . . . I knew, for a moment, that the only nightmare is the masochistic human mind.

Cross Creek, 357–58

I decided that nothing is more tangible for one's money than plumbing.

Cross Creek, 62

Spring

The business of the spring woods went forward leisurely in the golden morning. Red-birds were mating, and the crested males were everywhere, singing until Baxter's Island dripped with the sweetness of the sound.

The Yearling, 48

March came in with a cool and sunny splendor. The yellow jessamine bloomed late and covered the fences and filled the clearing with its sweetness. The peach trees blossomed, and the wild plums. The red birds sang all day, and when they had done with their song in the evening, the mocking birds continued. The ground doves nested and cooed to one another and walked about the sand of the clearing like shadows bobbing.

The Yearling, 384

They were instinct with life, the tight buds were aware of April, and if the stirring roots did not soon find foothold and nourishment, an orchard would die a-borning. With time to spare, it would have been best first to plow the entire acreage, but the loamy soil was

Rawlings in her Cross Creek flower garden, 1930s. Courtesy of the
Department of Special and Area Studies Collections, George A. Smathers
Libraries, University of Florida.

soft with spring, grass and weeds yet tender, and Ase began the digging of holes to receive the beginnings of trees.

The Sojourner, 55

The rough boat moved smoothly down the swift current. The run was broad at its upper reaches. The water was blue and the March sky over it was blue. A light wind stirred the white clouds. It was the kind of day he had always liked particularly. The banks were of a rosy red, for the swamp maple and the red-bud were in full spring color. Swamp laurel was in bloom and its sweetness filled the creek.

The Yearling, 412

A column of smoke rose thin and straight from the cabin chimney. The smoke was blue where it left the red of the clay. It trailed into the blue of the April sky and was no longer blue but gray. The boy Jody watched it, speculating.

The Yearling, 1

This spring one dove came ahead of time and flew inside my gate before the season ended. The laws of hospitality and refuge forbade my disturbing him and he took the overflow from the red-birds' feed basket unmolested. I am hypocrite enough in any case not to shoot at birds who live on my place.

Cross Creek, 249

A slow breeze stirred across the April night. The moonlight washed through the clearing in waves of warm silver.

South Moon Under, 177

He was dizzy with Spring. . . . His head was swimming with the strong brew made up of sun and the air and the thin gray rain. The flutter-mill had made him drunk.

The Yearling, 14

A soft rain fell in the night. The April morning that followed was clear and luminous. The young corn lifted pointed leaves and was six inches higher. The cow-peas in the field beyond were breaking the ground. The sugarcane was needle-points of greenness against the tawny earth. It was strange, Jody thought, whenever he had been away from the clearing, and came home again, he noticed things that he had never noticed before, but that had been there all the time. Young mulberries were clustered along the boughs. . . . The Scuppernong grapevine, a gift from his mother's kin in Carolina, was in bloom for the first time, and lace-like. The wild golden bees had found its fragrance, and were standing on their heads to guzzle its thin honey.

The Yearling, 74

I walk at sunset, east along the road. There are no houses in that direction, except the abandoned one where the wild plums grow, white with the bloom in spring-time.

Cross Creek, 5

A mark was on him from the day's delight, so that all his life, when April was a thin green and the flavor of rain was on his tongue, an old wound would throb and a nostalgia would fill him for something he could not quite remember. A whip-poor-will called across the bright night, and suddenly he was asleep.

The Yearling, 14–15

The early morning mist filled the valley. The willow trees along the stream lifted through it like cloaked and long-armed travelers rising from a night of sleep beside the water. The mist was milky, holding a subtle nourishment for the young leaves of maples and the pale timid buds of wild apples. Oak and beech and elm still brooded, leafless. The earth in late April was expectant. The winter wheat pushed up green spears anxiously, long confined by snow. A lone phoebe spoke from the woods, not quite singing.

The Sojourner, 46

Jody examined the deer hide. It was large and handsome, red with spring.

The Yearling, 72

He thought lazily now that it must now be April. Spring had taken over the scrub, and the birds were mating and singing in the bushes. Only he, in all the world, was homeless. He had been out in the world, and the world was a troubled dream, fluid and desolate, flanked by swamps and cypresses.

The Yearling, 422

The sun was dropping low in the west. Masses of white cloud hung above the flat marshy plain and seemed to be tangled in the tops of distant palms and cypresses. The sky turned orange, then saffron. . . . The season was more advanced than at the Creek, two hundred miles to the north, and I noticed that spring flowers were blooming among the lumpy hummocks. I leaned over to pick a white violet. There was a rattlesnake under the violet.

Cross Creek, 173

Place

Rawlings's Cross Creek farmhouse, 1939. Photograph by Eddie Davis. Courtesy of the Department of Special and Area Studies Collections, George A. Smathers Libraries, University of Florida.

There were affinities between men and places, recognizable, so that a man lived contentedly wherever, by his nature, he belonged.

Golden Apples, 307

Cross Creek is a bend in a country road, by land, and the flowing of Lochloosa Lake into Orange Lake, by water.

Cross Creek, 1

The matter of adjustment to physical environment is as fascinating as the adjustment of man to man, and as many-sided. The place that is right for one is wrong for another, and I think that much human unhappiness comes from ignoring the primordial relation of man to his background.

Cross Creek, 31

"It's a ——— blessing for us not many Yankees have seen country like this, or they'd move in on us worse than Sherman."

Zelma Cason, *Cross Creek*, 49

"Man, the scrub's a fine place to be. . . . If things ever gits too thick, you and me jest grab us each a young un and a handful o' shells and the guns and light out acrost it. I'd dare any man to mess up with me, yonder in the scrub."

Kezzy, *South Moon Under*, 333

The rain was more torrential than before. It poured down as though Juniper Creek and Silver Glen Run and Lake George and the St. John's River had all emptied over the scrub at once. The wind was no fiercer than before, but it was gusty. . . . It blew and rained and blew and rained and blew and rained.

The Yearling, 233

I do not understand how any one can live without some small place of enchantment to turn to. In the lakeside hammock there is a constant stirring in the tree-tops, as though on the stillest days the breathing of the earth is yet audible.

Cross Creek, 37

He loved the changing seasons in this place, from the first blood-root pushing through dank mould, to the last yellow poplar leaf bedded beneath the snow. He loved the March winds, the soft gray rain of April, the summer heat that shimmered visibly over golden wheat, the bleak gales of autumn, the winter ice that closed like a clean crystal death over field and wood. He wanted to know the seasons other-where, a wetter rain, a stronger sun, more sweeping storms and colder ice.

The Sojourner, 169

We need above all, I think, a certain remoteness from urban confusion, and while this can be found in other places, Cross Creek offers it with such beauty and grace that once entangled with it, no other place seems possible to us, just as when truly in love none other offers the comfort of the beloved.

Cross Creek, 3

The village exaggerates our differences and claims that something in the Creek water makes people quarrelsome. Our amenities pass unnoticed.

Cross Creek, 4

For myself, the Creek satisfies a thing that had gone hungry and unfed since childhood days. I am often lonely. Who is not? But I should be lonelier in the heart of a city.

Cross Creek, 5

The golden apples of Hesperides—The golden apples of Atalanta—Somewhere, the man remembered, he had been told the golden apple of mythology was an orange. For a moment he lost himself in antiquity. Here were ancient Greece and all of Persia. Here was old Seville. Here was Spain, starving, hoping, seeking, in Florida. Here were the magic isles, fruited with men's dreams.

Golden Apples, 236

Here in Florida the seasons move in and out like nuns in soft clothing, making no rustle in their passing. It is common for me at least to fall on a certain kind of sunny day into a sort of amnesia. I think with a start, "What is the time of year? Where was I yesterday? And is this May or October?"

Cross Creek, 243

A kind of spirit transcended race and nationality; found its peace in its own way; worked out its destiny in its own torment. For such, frontiers were not of place, but of the mind.

Golden Apples, 249

For learning a new territory and people as quickly as possible, I recommend taking the census on horseback.

Cross Creek, 48

Zelma is an ageless spinster resembling an angry and efficient canary. She manages her orange grove and as much of the village and country as needs management or will submit to it. I cannot decide whether she should have been a man or a mother. She combines the more violent characteristics of both and those who ask for or accept her ministrations think nothing of being cursed loudly at the very instant of being tenderly fed, clothed, nursed or guided through their troubles. She was the logical census taker for our district.

Cross Creek, 48–49

I came to Cross Creek with such a phobia against snakes that a picture of one in the dictionary gave me what Martha calls "the all-overs." I had the common misconception that in Florida they were omnipresent. I thought, "If anything defeats me, sends me back to urban civilization, it will be the snakes." They were not ubiquitous as I had expected, but I saw one often enough to keep my anxiety alive.

Cross Creek, 167

"I reckon you know, you got to be satisfied with a place to make out. And is you satisfied, then it don't make too much difference does you make out or no."

Martha Mickens, Cross Creek, 20

I found that in rural Florida, to refuse an invitation to a meal, if one is there at the time it is ready or nearly so, is to insult hospitality so grievously that the damage can seldom be repaired.

Cross Creek, 109

"But now the gov'mint is mighty pertickler in Caroliny and West Virginny. The revenooers is jest bounden determined nobody won't git to make none. But sho, they jest as good to stay to home and put their noses over their own pots. They cain't half ketch them fellers makin' moonshine up in them mountings. When they do come up with 'em, they're like to git buckshot in their breeches for their trouble. I mind me—"

Lantry, South Moon Under, 38

"If ever'body loved the same places, we'd be right over-crowded."

Penny, *The Yearling*, 243

His heart had awakened him, pounding in the night, from dreams of meeting stranger people, red, white, yellow, black and brown. In the dreams he sat with them beside their various hearth fires, sharing with them the alien foods of the encyclopedia, mysteriously communicating freely in alien tongues. He was half blind in his mind's eye from peering across the continent, and into the suns of foreign lands, and beyond them, beyond the Coral Sea and the Caribbean, to Europe and Iceland, Cape Horn and the newly discovered North Pole, past Africa and India, the Great Wall of China and forbidden Nepal and the steppes of Russia, into the Alps, the Andes and the Himalayas, and high above these, up into inter-stellar spaces, so dazzling that he might be unable to face it if he found it, the home he yearned for, the true and final home that was not and never had been nor could be, the old Linden farm near Peytonville.

The Sojourner, 265

"Cross Creek is the most queerest place and the queerest people I've ever known."

Samson, *Cross Creek*, 199

All delighted him, yet was alien. In the last hours across the thousands of miles of the beautiful, the fabulous nation, he understood that he had been watching so eagerly in the hope that he might recognize his home. It was not here. Neither had he left it behind him.

The Sojourner, 315

The test of beauty is whether it can survive close knowledge. This is as true of persons as of places.

Cross Creek, 245

"I came to Florida just to get away from Yankees."

MKR to Fred Tompkins, *Cross Creek*, 314

The road ran level for a way, rose a little, dipped down to the valley where the stream ran under a wooden bridge, wound its way four miles to the village of Peytonville, to the train, to the West, to the unknown and far away.

The Sojourner, 6

Long ago, before the Big Freeze, Florida was a tropic land of exile. Numbers of younger sons or ne'er-do-wells were sent here from England, subsidized to stay away. Some were given funds with which to establish orange groves, funds they often squandered. One of these, morose, ironic, must have come on this unknown, unsailed waterway. Bitter, perhaps, certainly home sick, he was struck by the deathly peace and the dark beauty; stirred by the pale water hyacinths, diaphanous and unearthly; and it was truly to him the River of Death, over which, once traversed, there is no crossing back again. Because this country had become as dear as life to me, the river held for me no horror. I wondered if the greater Styx might not be as darkly beautiful.

Cross Creek, 51

For this is an enchanted land.

Cross Creek, 7

Who Owns Cross Creek?

Who owns Cross Creek? The red-birds, I think, more than I, for they will have their nests even in the face of delinquent mortgages. And after I am dead, who am childless, the human ownership of grove and field and hammock is hypothetical. But a long line of red-birds and whippoorwills and blue-jays and ground doves will descend from the present owners of the nests in the orange trees, and their claim will be less subject to dispute than that of any human heirs. Houses are individual and can be owned, like nests, and fought for. But what of the land? It seems to me that the earth may be borrowed but not bought. It may be used, but not owned. It gives itself in response to love and tending, offers its seasonal flowering and fruiting. But we are tenants and not possessors, lovers and not masters. Cross Creek belongs to the wind and the rain, to the sun and the seasons, to the cosmic secrecy of seed, and beyond all, to time.

Cross Creek, 368

Acknowledgments

Special thanks are due to Meredith Babb at the University Press of Florida, both for her patient support of this project and for her long-standing commitment to maintaining Marjorie Kinnan Rawlings's presence in print. The editors are also very grateful to Flo Turcotte, the archivist of the Marjorie Kinnan Rawlings Papers at Smathers Library, University of Florida, Gainesville, for both her work and her assistance in procuring copies and permissions for the images in this volume that are held in the Rawlings archive. We also appreciate the help and guidance of the known and the unknown readers of the manuscript, whose careful consideration has resulted in this becoming a better book. To the members of the Rawlings Society, so many of whom have become such dear friends, the editors extend their most heartfelt thanks both for your friendship and for your own efforts to make sure that Rawlings's life is remembered and that her works will live on in eternity.

Works Cited

Acton, Patricia Nassif, Lady. *Invasion of Privacy: The "Cross Creek" Trial of Marjorie Kinnan Rawlings*. Gainesville: University Presses of Florida, 1988.

Glisson, J. T. *The Creek*. Gainesville: University Press of Florida, 1993.

Parker, Idella. *Idella: Marjorie Rawlings' "Perfect Maid."* With Mary Keating. Gainesville: University Press of Florida, 1992.

Rawlings, Marjorie Kinnan. *Blood of My Blood*. Edited by Anne Blythe Meriwether. Gainesville: University Press of Florida, 2002.

———. *Cross Creek*. New York: Scribners, 1942.

———. *Cross Creek Cookery*. New York: Scribners, 1942.

———. *Golden Apples*. New York: Scribners, 1935.

———. *Max and Marjorie: The Correspondence between Maxwell E. Perkins and Marjorie Kinnan Rawlings*. Edited by Rodger L. Tarr. Gainesville: University Press of Florida, 1999.

———. *Poems. Songs of a Housewife*. Edited by Rodger L. Tarr. Gainesville: University Press of Florida, 1997.

———. *The Private Marjorie: The Love Letters of Marjorie Kinnan Rawlings to Norton S. Baskin*. Edited by Rodger L. Tarr. Gainesville: University Press of Florida, 2004.

———. *Selected Letters of Marjorie Kinnan Rawlings*. Edited by Gordon Bigelow and Laura V. Monti. Gainesville: University Presses of Florida, 1983.

———. *Short Stories of Marjorie Kinnan Rawlings*. Edited by Rodger L. Tarr. Gainesville: University Press of Florida, 1994.

———. *The Sojourner*. New York: Scribners, 1953.

———. *South Moon Under*. New York: Scribners, 1932.

———. *The Uncollected Writings of Marjorie Kinnan Rawlings.* Edited by Rodger L. Tarr and Brent E. Kinser. Gainesville: University Press of Florida, 2007.

———. *When the Whippoorwill—.* New York: Scribners, 1940.

———. *The Yearling.* New York: Scribners, 1938.

Tarr, Rodger L. *Marjorie Kinnan Rawlings: A Descriptive Bibliography.* Pittsburgh: University of Pittsburgh Press, 1996.

Index

Brent E. Kinser is associate professor of English at Western Carolina University. He is the editor, with Rodger L. Tarr, of *The Uncollected Writings of Marjorie Kinnan Rawlings,* former coeditor of the *Marjorie Kinnan Rawlings Journal of Florida Literature,* and the current president of the Rawlings Society. In addition to his work on Rawlings, Kinser is the author of *The American Civil War in the Shaping of British Democracy* (2011), coordinating editor of *The Carlyle Letters Online*, an editor of *The Collected Letters of Thomas and Jane Welsh Carlyle*, and coeditor of *Carlyle Studies Annual.*

Rodger L. Tarr is a University Distinguished Professor Emeritus of English at Illinois State University. He is the editor of *Short Stories of Marjorie Kinnan Rawlings*; *Collected Poems of Marjorie Kinnan Rawlings*; *Max and Marjorie: The Correspondence between Maxwell E. Perkins and Marjorie Kinnan Rawlings; The Private Marjorie: The Love Letters of Marjorie Kinnan Rawlings to Norton S. Baskin; Marjorie Kinnan Rawlings: A Descriptive Bibliography,* and, with Brent E. Kinser, *The Uncollected Writings of Marjorie Kinnan Rawlings.*